I0133197

The Yoga Party:
Philosophical Writings

The Yoga Party: Philosophical Writings

Dedicated To My Wife Sandra

The Yoga Party: Philosophical Writings

I'd like to thank my friend Mark Perkins for being willing to take a look at an unknown writers work, reading this manuscript and giving me feedback.

I'd also like to thank Professor Tom Weston who has been very supportive of my endeavors over the years for taking a look at this and giving me valuable feedback.

Table of Contents

The Yoga Party: Philosophical Writings

Introduction

This is the first book of three. Firstly this book is Philosophical Writings, next is Poetry and last is Political Writings. The unifying theme to this series is the Yoga Party, ultimately a political party which emphasizes a state of mind.

In writing this book many basic philosophical principles are included. Those without a background in philosophy might want to brush up on basic philosophical thought, although I don't feel it is impossible for someone to digest most of what is here with minimal preparation. The Donald Palmer books are entertaining and accessible. Most important I think is to keep an open mind when looking at the analysis. For those that wish to dive right in without any preparation I will identify some basic philosophical principles.

First of all philosophy is as old as humans have lived on this earth. Contrary to many professors of philosophy in the west, different philosophical positions exist worldwide which all contribute interesting perspectives to world thought. The study of western academic philosophy traditionally has largely ignored non-western philosophical traditions. Part of this definitely relies on a sort of feeling of superiority of this thought by some. This is changing somewhat now and non-western positions in some ways have penetrated western philosophy, although most of this penetration is based on philosophers borrowing from the non-western thought and adopting them as their own.

This book will not attempt to do this. I attempt in this book to approach the dominant world philosophical positions as being equal in value. But that is not to say that each traditions contribution to thought is the same. Ultimately though there are many more similarities between different philosophical positions than is often thought. All people have the same impulse to understand the reasons for the way things are and in doing so provide them some degree of comfort in understanding these things.

The stepping off point depends on the teachings of Sri Aurobindo. This 20th century master applied his interpretation of Hinduism to western thought. I attempt to present an interpretation that largely accords with Aurobindo yet ultimately rejects many of his tenets. For example his presentation of disembodied spirits runs counter to my rationalistic perspective.

Looking at Eastern and Western thought one finds many basic differences. In India for example where Aurobindo was born the prevailing attitude is that that which is most real is spirit while in the west we find attitudes about matter predominate. Aurobindo tries to find linkage between spirit and matter which I expand upon. I believe that Aurobindo's thought can be used as a critique of western thought as well as identifying dogmas inherent in eastern thought.

The predominant problem in the west lies in the confusion between metaphysics and epistemology. Metaphysics deals with the nature of reality while epistemology is involved in finding theories of knowledge. What we know and what there is can be very different things. What we know (e.g., epistemology) is useful but what is (e.g., metaphysics) is not necessarily known. In western society there is some confusion between these two aspects of western thought. Scientists often identify that which is known with that which is real. The gist seems to be that that which is real is only that which can be known. Only things that can be known can be considered when talking about the world, and if we don't know something or can't describe it then this is considered nonsense. Unfortunately this results in a very myopic view of the world.

If being myopic were the only sin of modern western thought then this would be something that we could all live with. But this perspective has some profound ramifications which are discussed at length within. Ultimately the way we see ourselves determines the way we see the world. A cultures bias is largely determined by their creation myths.

Humans need certainty in their lives in order to live an existence which minimizes anxiety. In order to feel comfortable we must assert our importance, our essence, our existence as being vital in the universe. But one curse of being free is the ability to investigate phenomenon with an open mind and to examine things which seem impossible or fantastic. For if we are free at all as a gift or curse from God we must exercise this quality be it for better or worse.

But hopefully broadening one's outlook and keeping an open mind will enable one to examine things that before one thought not possible. It's hard to see the forest from the trees but if we look hard enough and far enough we can find a place for ourselves there. So journey on and don't tarry for the world is there for all to see and rends itself apparent in all our senses and minds. Journey on and see what there is to see. For to do otherwise is to waste our most prized asset, that of being fully human and fully conscious. Socrates said "The unexamined life is not worth living." Don't go through your life as you are lost in a cloud but consider the great ideas of your time and also the new ideas that are just now being born.

Introduction to the Yoga Party

The Yoga Party is a political party. It is intended to be an alternative to the status quo. Certainly much of the world is being politicized and westernized. But with the interchange between East and West it is inevitable that the West too will be changed. The question comes up, how can a philosophy, a way of life be politicized? Politics is part of everyone's existence. It's part of how we understand ourselves and the world. It also is a way that we order society so that it can function properly. In this manner it is part and parcel of the human experience, and nothing permeates the human existence than its understanding of a common unity between us all.

The Yoga Party preaches no political dogma. The Yoga Party only wants all to find their most fully realized existence. No one is excluded from the Yoga Party. No one is shown preference or is marginalized. This is because ultimately we are composed of the same, let's call it spiritual matter. What is spiritual matter you might ask? Well let's save that for a later time. Suffice it to say that this spiritual matter of which we all belong shares in the trial and tribulations of the material existence. Having this in common all share the same stake in our destiny, rich and poor, black and white, male and female, even plants and animals.

This is a party of peace. No violence dwells here. But also we are joined in a unity of being. Being sentient beings we all suffer. According to Aurobindo this suffering masks our higher nature of joy and bliss. Nevertheless in our material existence we all dwell in the darkness of the Socratic cave. We are tortured by our thoughts, feelings, hopes and dreams. Certainly we are happy, at least we like to think there is some satisfaction in life, but it is all too common that we wonder why me? How come I made that mistake, why did that person leave me? Why did my love die? Therefore we all share this common bond.

The materialist West emphasizes the material relations of existence, especially private property. We are taught to worship the rich and often the newly rich are referred to as "stars" that shine so brightly bathing us in their light. Role models are paraded by, shaping our attitudes and our existence. Yet when we realize we are all the product of the primordial stew and have a common stake in our existence, we come to realize rich or poor we share a common bond. We are indoctrinated with the idea that those that are wealthier are happier; have more satisfying love. Perhaps, but with the fulfillment of these desires comes an even greater suffering when these bonds fail.

The Yoga Party is not a fundamentalist religious party.

We have no religious dogma, nor profess any standards to which one must adhere, nor do its adherents claim to be holy in any sense. We do not claim the moral high ground; neither do we try to save someone after their ethical lapses. The Yoga Party does not serve as a model for others to emulate. Its members can worship or not anyway they wish to worship, be conservative, independent, liberal or socialist. One important tenet of the Yoga Party is that there is a spiritual aspect to life. But the way spirit is understood is different than is commonly thought.

This spiritual aspect to life does not imply a personification of God, but worshiping a personification of God does not exclude one from membership. In fact this spiritual aspect does not imply the existence of a God at all. God fearing and atheists alike can be member of the Yoga Party. The Yoga Party does not have a church yet we all may worship, yet who, what or where we worship depends on our individual preferences.

It matters not whether those members of the Yoga Party worship Yahweh, Jehovah, Krishna, Buddha, Allah, Nature, Consciousness, Bliss, Trees, Clouds, The Sky, Chaos, Negation, Emptiness, Love, Flowers, Harmony and any other life affirming principles wherever we may find them.

The Yoga Party avoids dogma that promotes destruction. As Jesus said we may know what something is by the fruit it bears. The Yoga Party avoids dogma that is parochial, cut off from other people's wants, needs, desires, hopes, dreams, and happiness. The Yoga Party avoids worldviews that embrace bigotry, support injustice, xenophobia, racism, sexism, classism, hatred, avarice, insensitivity.

Most agree and I feel all can be persuaded that there is a spiritual basis to our existence. An atheist might object to the "spirit" but even the atheist would agree that there are natural forces that drive all that exists and ceases to exist. God can be thought of as being an apt creator, lover, just law giver or as being amorphous, ubiquitous, unknown, known, natural, individual, organismic, cosmological, supernatural, empty, nothingness, love, eroticism, singularity.

The Yoga party spreads a wide tent, not unlike other political parties, but we do not share a political platform other than to promote that which results in the development of the highest physical functioning, mental acuity, wholeheartedness, and breadth of consciousness understanding, that this is all part and parcel of what we call spirit.

The Yoga Party abhors violence

The Yoga Party does not abhor death. Death is not a desired end, but neither is it to be shunned. As all live, all must die. For finite existence to be a manifestation of the infinite, both must embrace both life and death.

Death is not to be a source of delight nor a state of dejection. Those that delight in death are purveyors of death. Those that embrace death find their nature in the absolute. Death must be accepted.

The purveyors of death serve a function of allowing things to find their own way. The absolute can only be realized, can only become cognizant of itself if there is a spirit in which to behold it. This beholding is the function of a spiritual being. The purveyors of death are like a stagnant pool, which is finally met by the flowing sea. Only through embracing our spiritual nature can we surmount the evils of those that delight in death.

Much is said about the distinction between the saying "an eye for an eye" or "if someone strikes you turn the other cheek." The Yoga party does find a time to deal an eye for an eye only if the eye is the eye of wanton destruction, but the Yoga Party always abhors violence.

The earth cares little if humans fail or even all life fails, but the spirit of matter can not come to know its true nature if life perishes. Yet what we call life is different from what is ordinarily thought.

Turning the other cheek does not imply abject servility. There are no masters and no servants in domain of the absolute, all participate in its manifestation of activity. The purveyors of death dwell in insularity, bound by the blindness of ignorance.

The Yoga Party is not a party to pacifism, but it is in no manner a party of violence. Violence is only a human invention to justify injustice. Violence results from seeing oneself as composed of mind dwelling in senseless matter. Violence results from seeing the ego as separate from the divine spirit. This clouded perspective, oblivious to spirit, produces selfish annihilation.

The Yoga Party is opposed to all violence but recognizes that the ashes of death fertilize the seeds of a new generation of spirit. Only by avoiding selfish action; genocide, persecution, injustice, murder, and torture, can the ashes of death provide a fertile ground for the fruits of enlightenment.

The Yoga Party does not embrace transcendentalism but practices action

The Yoga Party does not embrace transcendentalism. The Yoga Party is a party of action. Rulers can be tyrants, benefactors, paternalistic, or hollow. The Yoga Party acts for the benefit of all people. The party recognizes that tyranny precedes freedom, that oppression precedes revolution, ignorance precedes wisdom.

Only through action can one's self nature be realized. Only through movements can people tread the path of vision. A materialist may ask, what does the Yoga Party say to me? A materialist believes when one dies all ceases. As it is said "ashes to ashes dust to dust". But if one's life perishes, then what was that life in the first place? If life is transient then what constitutes life? Is life only something one knows while they live? If life is not knowable outside of life then how can life be real at all? This reduces the materialist to an idealist, something that they would fervently object.

Yet as an ideal life never ends; the struggles of the world have no meaning. If all is ideal then matter has no substance, life does not flourish, a life without goals, without love, without meaning, without virtue, without knowledge. Yet all these things exist and more because if they didn't exist then something would be lacking, Being would be an inert mass of hollow stuff.

So the Yoga Party lives in the world and dwells in the infinite. The Yoga party embraces wisdom, love, virtue in the world as a manifestation of the world bound up in birth and death, struggle, and righteousness. The hammer of consciousness is honed on the anvil of corporeality; by throwing oneself into the machinations of existence, one is transformed, the world is uplifted and a new age is born.

So where does the Yoga Party begin? Does it begin with brute force? Does it begin pondering the imponderables? Or does it begin by removing the blindness that binds us, not only educating ourselves but others, thus eliminating action without a foundation, thought without manner. As a being moving through time in the timeless eternity, we constitute eternity in an infinite pass dissolved to nothingness and therefore we must live for the present, to rectify our misjudgments about people and the world and ourselves and to reach out to others to join us in this noble enterprise, a search for the principles of matter and energy, of consciousness and light. Light the flame in the darkness and show others the way.

The Yoga Party is a Party of Unity

Some perhaps are expecting a call to action, or at least how we understand a political party, as an organization that organizes and such. But in fact in order for this party to work under a common umbrella we must agree on some sort of dogma (i.e., systems of understanding) of which we can all agree. This is more important than might appear at face value. We take for granted our beliefs in the West, which are very different from what we have in other parts of the world.

Not only do those in the West not understand other non-Western belief systems, but they often are not really aware of their own. They have what I call the "can't see the forest from the trees" syndrome.

You may not be convinced that it is necessary to have a distinct awareness of oneself for an organization, especially a political party, but it is the party dogma that is essential in forming a viable system in which all can participate. We all must find common principles on which we all can agree. Ultimately we all are human and deal with the same human problems, food, shelter, comfort etc.

It is only through finding our commonalities that we can make this party effective. As John Lennon once said about revolution that we need only need to "change [our] minds instead."

So the Yoga Party ultimately is about synthesis, at least our understanding of this synthesis. Only then can we have a big tent where all can dwell.

But perhaps even more important is to realize that in fact we are the All, and therefore the synthesis of All. Understanding this helps us arrive at an understanding of ourselves, of others and of all that is.

The Yoga Party is about the synthesis of all. Only then can we find true unity. The Yoga Party is a party of unity.

The Yoga Party Is Not Hindu In Any Sense

The Yoga Party is not Hindu or Indian in any sense. It is referred to as the Yoga Party because the word Yoga is derived from "yoke" which means to join together. All are welcome in the Yoga Party; it refers not to country, religion, ethnicity, etc. The Yoga

Party is considered to be the place where all can take refuge if they so feel and in doing so, it is hoped, reach their full potential.

The Yoga Party is not Hindu or Indian in any sense, because the system adapted from Aurobindo, is universal and therefore not limited. It is not even a party of humans simply, but embraces all life and all of creation.

No system of beliefs runs contrary to the system of the Yoga Party, although people may believe it does. This is largely because of ignorance regarding the principles of the Yoga Party, as well as misunderstanding about the nature of the Infinite in their own belief systems.

The Yoga Party does not recognize a genealogy of Gods, nor does it recognize their multiplicity because the all – Being is one. This does not conflict with other seekers of truth because the Yoga Party adopts no religious dogma and therefore cannot be drawn into conflict with ones own belief system.

As stated before, the Yoga Party is not a religion at all but emphasizes spirituality. This does not mean that the Yoga Party necessarily recognizes an "inspiration of self", but rather simply that all is spirit as all is the result of creation.

Even in an infinite never-ending universe all can be called spirit, because all that is finite exists through infinity and therefore has an eternal substance. All in some manner must be the creation of the infinite and eternal. This too is what I call spirit.

The Yoga Party has influence through unity. Through the bond of humankind, recognizing the importance of all things, can one stand together to face the scourge of those that see the egoistic self as a means and an end, not recognizing their true nature.

Only when recognizing one's true interests can one act in the interests of all. This is the goal of the Yoga Party, to act in the interests of all and to neglect no one. Only then will people see their true interests.

Only when people see the unity of spirit as the activity of the eternal can one recognize ones own self interests. This comes through understanding the truth that all religions are one and that the Yoga Party is not provincial, ethnic, or parochial. Simply by us being yoked together can we understand our true interests. Only through unity can we understand our strength. This is a strength that comes about not through violence but through peace and solidarity, calmness in struggle, equipoise in action.

Let it be clearly stated: The Yoga Party is not Hindu in any sense. Not in any shape, way or form.

Jnana Yoga is not a Religious Practice.

Jnana Yoga is not a religious practice. This is the philosophical like yoga.

There are in fact many Yogas which include Bhakti Yoga which is where you give devotion to God. Christianity is a Bhakti Yoga. Jnana Yoga is very different.

One might wonder how you can separate Bhakti Yoga from Jnana Yoga since they are both Yoga. Yoga includes both the head and the heart. Humans are bound and act through both. One feels with the heart (metaphorically speaking) and one also thinks with the head. Would one say one was not a Yogi because they cared about humanity deeply and at the same time understood the nature of human kind?

Sri Aurobindo talks about the unity of the Yoga's in his Integral Synthesis as well it should. We are not simply heart but also mind. Understanding God is not enough. One also can experience the bliss of consciousness through the passage to the Godhead.

xxi

Jnana Yoga is one of the paths to God. It is the most like philosophy. But instead of trying to understand a particular epistemology (e.g., theory of knowledge) or metaphysics (nature of reality) based in specific applications, one tries to find the epistemology of Being (the godhead) and the metaphysics of Being. When one can understand the nature of the all of All, then one can understand the ultimate, the cosmos and the Being of humankind.

This does not really involve talking about God at all, at least not in the western sense. One could just as easily call it the Ultimate or the All.

Traditional Hindu Yoga makes a critical mistake. It calls the world illusory. While one's vision may be unfocused, even in our state of conscious poverty we perceive the supreme. There is no illusion here, only limitation. But the limitation is not what is essential in human beings for the true self is the ultimate. How could the ultimate dwell in something that was totally blind? If this were true there could be no manifestation of Being in the world. The blindness comes from our limited perspective, being bound to the senses one only gets the sensual aspect of existence. And we are bound to the senses.

Sri Aurobindo makes it clear that the human existence is every bit as real as the ultimate and this is because the human existence in some sense is the ultimate or God. For if human existence were not real, pure consciousness would not be possible. But a "life divine" is possible.

So in examining the nature of God or Being speculatively one can enhance consciousness. It seems with this study one can increase consciousness and actually become enlightened. But it is important to realize that to be enlightened one must escape or at least develop an alternate mode of self which embodies pure experience. This is fundamentally different from speculative reason.

The ecstasy of the religious is well documented when beholding God. But God can be a deity for some, but for the Jnana Yogist the ultimate is that which sheds light on the manifold as well as the unity of existence.

It seems quite likely that the Jnana Yogist would rather experience the flash of insight rather than the bliss of rapture. This is because the Jnana Yogist dwells in the mind and not the heart. This flash of insight or consciousness serves to unite oneself with that which one is already. This is what gives the study of Jnana Yoga it's satisfaction as well as philosophy in general. But it is questionable if the flash of pure consciousness will ever come. Perhaps then this is something that must be found through an integral yoga.The understanding of Pure Being only satisfies a few and is unattainable by most.

This then is why I say Jnana Yoga is not religious.

The General Strike is the Primary Tool of the Yoga Party

The general strike is the primary tool for political change in the Yoga Party. The action of a general strike is a profound moving force and if practiced with the solidarity of all cannot fail.

Street protest is not necessary or even called for. Street protests can result in exposure, violence and arrest. Through provocation from the police or the excesses of the demonstrators, the values of a movement can become harmed. Participating in a mass demonstration can make oneself vulnerable to arrest, perhaps long term imprisonment and a subsequent record.

With the reported construction of prison camps, use of chemical and biological agents, it is recommended by the Yoga Party that one does not demonstrate and thus expose themselves to harm. The method of the general strike is as effective or even more effective, it lowers ones visibility and when practiced in common can bring a state to its knees.

One advantage of the general strike is that violence is not an option. Since you are not involved in an active demonstration and not exposed to harm (i.e., tear gas, beatings, taser, water cannon, clubs etc.) then not only will your well-being be protected but also you will be spared the emotional turmoil that accompanies such events, and using the general strike instead prevents these emotions from having negative consequences for yourself and others.

One of the first things to do is to turn off the TV. The TV, being an organ of the state, will be used to humiliate, discredit, and in anyway possible harm the general strike. As seems obvious, those that watch TV will most likely not be involved in or support the general strike.

The general strike can be useful in many ways. For example I am not going to turn on any electricity on the days of the strike. I

1

purchased candles to use instead of electricity. I will not turn on
my computer. I will not drive my car. I will not talk on the phone. I
will not purchase anything on this day. Because the ruler depends
on production and consumption this cannot fail.

Acting according to this method may not seem to be very
effective, at least not as effective as marching in the streets, but in
fact it is much more effective. This action does not involve one in
danger to ones life and health. It does not expose one to arrest. It
does not expose one to be identified as a subversive or domestic
"terrorist" which could result in unforeseen consequences. This
also will preserve your own integrity because you will maintain
your solemn peaceful attitude with compassion and love for all
without being drawn into the arena of vindictiveness and strife.

The effectiveness of the general strike of course depends upon
the solidarity of the masses; as individuals though it is important
because one is standing up for ones principles. Not much is lost
and little is put at risk. On the other hand if the people en masse
support and act in unison to a general strike, the result will be
momentous and negative consequences do not seem possible. The
world will change. Either way, acting as a mass movement or
acting individually is important. You have stood up for your ideals
and even if alone you show others that you are earnest in your
beliefs, and that your beliefs lead to action. You are showing
others that the goal of the general strike is what you believe in and
in participating in the general strike you are showing others that
this is what you value and therefore are showing that, in your view
at least, that a general strike is what all should adopt.

Only through peace, compassion, insight and solidarity can the
Yoga Party be successful. If it was otherwise then its goals would
be self-defeating. If one were to resort to violence, hate and
destruction then the goals would become that which the rulers are
trying to defeat. It would be the old story of the failed state

overthrown to only have installed another ruthless dictator. What sort of advantage could be derived from this?

While counteraction is possible against the general strike, it seems that it must be muted. While the government may control the organs of states, its people are its life blood. Without the circulation of commerce and capital the organism must die. While in a general strike the state might threaten action against the strikers, this would be like cutting ones body off from the head to save the head, this is not possible.

Of course in a general strike the leaders will be hunted for, not only to stop the strike, but to strike fear into the strikers that they might be next – to set an example of what might happen to them.

Even under the circumstances of a general strike then there is some risk, but be brave for a new day is coming. Stand together in unity as we are in fact one. Only when the evil state is no longer able to function can we the people take control and lead the state down a path toward a hopeful future rather than the present path of despair. But when the evil state collapses, their hatred must be accepted as a sense of loss and we must recognize that they too have suffered and are deserving of love and compassion.

Be strong for the path is not clearly defined and the hazard along the way cannot be seen from the distance. But practice forbearance because the flowers of the tree will blossom and the fruit will ripen and fall. Be vigilant and true.

If you cannot participate in the general strike then at least turn off your TV. This is the least you can do. And if possible turn it off forever and learn to read. This is the best present you can give to yourself and others. This too is a very important form of action against any evil state.

The general strike is the primary tool of the Yoga Party.

The Nature of Modern Religion

I often have had a difficult time convincing students that comparative religion is not in fact a religion course. Yet the way many Comparative Religion courses are taught make it seem like a religion course. Not only that but the title of these courses "Comparative Religion" often seem to do no comparison at all. Oftentimes students in comparative religion courses get a hodgepodge of information on different religions without finding the elements that are common to all religions as well as basic elements that differ.

A comparative religion course should show no preference for any religious perspective. Also since comparative religion is a philosophy course, judgments should be avoided, as judgments are part of moral thinking. The primary objective of such a course is not to enhance moral thinking although this would be a desirable byproduct, instead comparative religion should be quasi-historical. One cannot avoid the influence of history on the world's great religions. But also, and most importantly, one should talk about what contributions the different world religions have made to different societies and the world as a whole.

Religions are born, change shape and perish depending on earthly pressures. As should be obvious, most religions no longer exist and the ones that do exist commonly have modified their dogma over time to adapt to the influences of their times.

To discuss all of the world's religions would of course be impossible. What I have set out to do here is to present the religions that have had the most influence in human history which are predominant in modern times. It should be stated though that if a religion is not listed here this does not mean that the religion is any less valuable, that its tenets are any less important; but it is necessary to set some limits on this endeavor in order to complete the study.

The religions I will be talking in this introduction about include the Abrahamic religions which include Judaism, Christianity, and Islam. Also discussed will be the predominately Asian religions of Hinduism, Buddhism, Taoism and Confucianism.

In doing this I will avoid a piecemeal approach. Comparative Religion should be less about the religious experience and more about understanding how they are different and how they are similar and how even it might be considered that they overlap. To do this I will be defining certain concepts, for example monotheism (one God). We can use the concept of monotheism to describe the Abrahamic religions but also to describe Hinduism which is fundamentally different. While being alike in that the two traditions are monotheistic, in the Abrahamic religions its adherents have a personal relationship with God while in Hinduism the understanding of God is very impersonal. These difference and others like it help flesh out the differences, similarities as well as the syncretistic aspects of different religions.

The Religions that you are probably most familiar with are the Abrahamic religions. The Abrahamic religions include the Judaic, Christian and Islamic traditions. These religions generally worship a personal God. The Asian religions on the other hand have an impersonal understanding of God or Being. These traditions include Hinduism, indirectly Buddhism, and Taoism. Also there is a belief system that is often considered a religion and has great influence in China called Confucianism which rests on social teachings and morality which I will talk about later.

As it is difficult for those who accept the Abrahamic religions to understand the Asian religions, so to is it difficult for the Asian traditions to understand the Abrahamic traditions. There is an old saying that "you can't see the forest from the trees." Just as we take our belief system for granted so too do people in other parts of the world take their own for granted. These different perspectives constitute and determine the fundamental attitudes we have toward the world whether we realize it or not.

In order to understand other belief systems we need to be able to understand our own. In order to do this it is useful to look at our own belief systems first, to understand how we understand them so that we are able to look at foreign belief systems so as to understand how they differ.

What does it mean to have a "personal" relationship with God? We hear this often in churches but what does this mean from a philosophical perspective? God in the Abrahamic religions is the creator of the cosmos, the creator of the world and of people themselves. There is a sharp division between God who creates all things and the thing that God has created. Because of this God is separate from his creation. God the Creator is all powerful and this is ostensibly demonstrated by the creation of all that is. On the other hand the world seems limited and finite. Human Beings are certainly finite, subject to the whims of nature, being born, grow to adulthood, to old age and finally death. Our nature is very limited unlike Gods.

This difference between God and ourselves has allowed us to have an individual identity separate from God. Because of this separateness and independence we are able to make our own decisions, and are therefore responsible for our own actions. We are not bound by God in any manner, but we are devout, we pay homage to God and pray often in Gods name. When we pray to God we are praying to an "other". It can be said when we are praying that we are having a "personal" relationship with God. This idea of distance from our creator enables us to live in the world as free beings.

On the other hand in the Asian religions, while there is a creative force (in Taoism the potentiate is called Non-Being and in Hinduism it is called Brahma). Human life is not separate from the

6

essence of the "All" (i.e., God, or Being, or the Void or the Divine) and the creative aspects of God are only manifestations of the eternal God, that is the "All" of all.

This is very difficult for those from the Abrahamic tradition to understand. In the Abrahamic religions the cognitive distance between God and humans enables humans to think clearly with an emphasis on rationality, in the Asian religions we "are" God (e.g., Hinduism) or Buddha (e.g., in Buddhism) or the natural result of the potential of Non-Being, that constitutes Being in Taoism. In Taoism Being is not really being separate from Non-Being but rather that Non-Being is the potential aspect and Being is the actual aspect of the "All" (e.g., in Taoism).

We cannot separate ourselves in the Asian traditions from the Divine. Since we are at our very essence that which is Divine or Godly in our own being, then we cannot "reach out" to the eternal Divine because we already are the Divine. Therefore, like a person that cannot have a relationship with themselves (i.e., it would be meaningless to pat ourselves on the back and say hello), we then have what is called an "impersonal" relationship with the Divine (I.e., we are already the Divine as all things are the Divine).

This then is a jumping off point for understanding the difference between the Abrahamic Religions and the Asian Traditions.

<u>The Triads of Religion</u>

There are commonalities in the Christianity, Hinduism, Taoism. All of these religions talk about a triad of existence. Also in China there is a different sort of triad where an individual believer often embraces Buddhism, Taoism and Confucianism in a sort of singular belief system. Even in Taoism itself there is a trinity composed of the philosophical aspects, the religious aspects and its meditative aspects.

In Christianity there is the trinity. The parts of the trinity are the Father, Son and Holy Ghost. In the trinity the Father is the transcendental Deity. The Son is Jesus Christ. The Holy Ghost is a sort of divine inspiration in the world. The position of the trinity is not followed by the Abrahamic religion Islam.

Similarly in Hinduism, also a monotheistic religion, we have Brahma (the creator), Vishnu (the preserver) and Shiva (the destroyer). These are all, like the trinity and God in Christianity, consubstantial with Brahman (the "All" of all) in the Vedantic Hindu tradition. In Taoism there is Non-Being (e.g., the potential aspect of Being), Being (e.g., the actual aspect of Being) and the 10,000 things (e.g., things of the world which ultimately informs ethical systems).

These three major divisions what I will call Trinitarian traditions have many interesting similarities. In Christianity God created the heavens and the earth and all things that are in it. In Hinduism too Brahma is a creator that has created all things. And in Taoism an aspect of creation springs forth from Non-Being. Although in this case Non-Being is not a creator in a theistic sense (e.g., Non-Being is not God but is more like a natural process). Explaining the existence of all there is, the argument that "Why is there something rather than nothing?" is a problem that has faced all peoples of the worlds. All religions have creation myths of one sort or another. And since there is a creator it also seems necessary to have that which is created.

Christianity and the Abrahamic religions in general drive a sharp wedge between the Creator and the created. All of the powers of God are generally limited to his transcendental realm although it is thought by many that God intervenes in the world during periods of great sin by his human children. Also angels can have great power in the world which includes Satan. Satan has no relation to God except that he was one of God's angels who were cast out.

Humans lack all of the power of God with the exception of the Son of God Jesus. Otherwise this distinction between the created and the creator holds tight. God is wholly transcendent and humans are wholly immanent.

On the other hand in Vedantic Hinduism God (Brahman) is all there is. The ultimate Brahman is not part of the Hindu trinity and subsumes it. Or for that matter the Hindu trinity is not part of Brahman. The ultimate Brahman has no parts.

Hinduism would not claim to be polytheistic because of it's thousands of God's any more that Christianity would claim to be polytheistic because of the trinity. Jesus is unique. No other human beings could be God. This is reserved for his son and only his son Jesus.

Yet in Hinduism there are no hard lines between the creator Brahma (notice this is different from Brahman) and Brahma's creation. Brahman is transcendental but also Brahman is worldly as well. While Christianity has the difficulty of explaining how God can be all parts of the trinity, for instance in Jesus' case both all human and all God, Hinduism has the difficulty in explaining how God can be the "ALL" of all and yet be responsible for all the different changes that occur in the world. Where does cause and effect come in? If you are everything then how can you be something?

9

Taoism then is the last triad discussed. As mentioned before there is Non-Being, Being and the things of the world (e.g., "the 10,000 things). While we can have a sort of an idea of what it means to be "ALL" in Hinduism, or to be Yahweh in the Judeo-Christian tradition, Non-Being seems to be a mysterious concept. We can have some comprehension of what "Being" might be and have intimate knowledge of the 10,000 things but how can we understand Non-Being?

This concept is not so different from the Christian God's Omnipotence. We cannot really understand intuitively how something can be omnipotent but we consider Yahweh to be so. In Hinduism too the existence of Brahman cannot be understood except to say that it is. Like these traditions Non-Being is unknowable and can only be talked about metaphorically. The fundamental work of Taoism is the book by mystic Lao Tzu called the Tao Te Ching or translated, "The Way and It's Power." Ultimately aspects of all three (e.g., Non-Being, Being and the 10,000 things) are transcendent and paramount.

Unlike Christianity and like Hinduism, there is no sharp distinction between that which creates (e.g., Non-Being) and that which it creates (e.g., Being) or for that matter the world (e.g., the 10,000 things). Whether Taoism and Hinduism are indeed different in nature with regards to deities is open to question. While philosophical Taoism says nothing about God's or deities and Hinduism has thousands of deities, there is a branch of Taoism called religious Taoism or folk Taoism which accepts a plethora of Gods.

Nevertheless philosophical Taoism is the most naturalistic of the religions. Some would consider it bordering on pantheism (e.g., God as the aggregate of all nature). Unlike Hinduism there is no supremacy of the Absolute. Non-Being is no more foundational than Being or the 10,000 things, they work in a sort of homeostatic motion and therefore interact with each aspect and in essence are

10

not really different from each other at all. In Hinduism by contrast, most often the world is considered to be illusory and only that which is most real is the Ultimate and Absolute Brahman.

These then are some fundamental differences between Christianity, Hinduism and Taoism.

The Conceivable

That which is conceivable is possible. If it were not possible then it would not be conceivable.

It is conceivable that one can change lead into gold. It is conceivable that one can right wrongs done.

But it is not conceivable that one both turns left and right at the same time. Or that one lies and tells the truth at the same time. Or that circles are squares or that blue is red.

An example one of my cherished professors provided was that time travel is impossible. If one were to travel into the past and meet themselves, albeit younger; that this was impossible. You cannot be yourself and another at the same time so time travel is impossible. This is not conceivable.

It is then true that one can use human reason to understand the world. The philosopher Lucretius was famous for this. But if we say God exists, is that conceivable? If we do not know God as God, can we say that God exists unless you consider God as that which is unknowable? It is my assertion that God is knowable. Notice the difference between the word unknown and unknowable. The first means not known and the other is not able to be known.

So then can we say the unknown exists? If it is not known we cannot know it to exist. But the question is is it conceivable that the unknown can exist? To this the answer must be of course yes! We don't know about new species that scientists discover all the time, but they do exist. We are constantly discovering new worlds which we knew nothing of before. But even if God is unknown God is knowable in principle. That is God is conceivable. That is the project of Jnana Yoga.

While Jnana Yoga can be an aid in understanding God the unknown, this knowledge is more than rational and can result in an enhanced consciousness.

Further study is useful and is in fact necessary to understand the scope of the Yoga Party and reading this book would hopefully help understanding this project. One thing I find hard to decide is that, if the dogma in Shankara, a famous Indian non-dualist, and Jnana Yoga in general is a form of speculative reasoning run rampant as Kant warned against? The atheist claims that you cannot claim to know something that you cannot know through experience. Something is not knowledge if it cannot be falsified in principle according to the skeptic. This is useful in science, and in fact this is essential, but then we also find ourselves living in the shadow of Plato's cave.

This is why Raja Yoga is important. The experience of the One is the evidence, not unlike the rapture of the Saints. These trances have been shown to change the type of brainwaves exhibited and has a certain calming effect.

The Paths of Yoga and Synthesis

Yoga is more than doing amazing things with your body, although that too is included in what is referred to as Yoga. In the parlance it is referred to as Hatha Yoga. This Yoga has become very popular in the West as a health exercise. One reason this part of Yoga has caught on is because Yoga as a form of exercise is it is easy to understand by the health conscious and it is undeniable that practicing Hatha Yoga is very beneficial. But Hatha Yoga is not where it ends at all. All the practices I'm going to list are useful in acquiring God consciousness, where Hatha Yoga serves as a good preparation for the other types of Yoga.

Most are familiar with Raja Yoga. A famous ancient teacher of Raja Yoga is Pantanjali. This involves going into a deep meditative state. This is what we usually think of when we see a Siddhi sitting cross legged, perhaps with some beads in one hand in a state of deep meditation. Studies have been done that show that Yogi's can control the autonomic nervous system, slow the heart beat and change their brains waves. It is with this meditation where the claim is made of telepathy and clairvoyance.

Then there is Karma Yoga. This yoga is basically living your life so as to not accumulate any bad karma which will increase your karmic "baggage" and result in further rebirth. Usually a practitioner of Karma yoga performs each activity without any end in mind; for example for wealth, power or status, but simply as tribute to God or Brahman. There is no heaven or hell here, only rebirth which one wants to escape. Ones understanding of the self is limited. When one escapes rebirth, they are no longer individuals, but become simply aware without karma.

Next is Bhakti Yoga. This yoga is done with devotion to God. In this respect it is like Christianity and one could say from the outside looking in that Christianity is a form of Bhakti Yoga. A

14

personal God is worshiped. This is different from what we mean by Brahman, because Brahman is individual, natural and transcendent at the same time. It's not that God is different, only the way of understanding God is. Finally there is Jnana Yoga. It is rather like philosophy and involves speculative reason.

Take for example this metaphor. One way one can think of these 4 different approaches to Yoga is that one needs to think of someone on a journey. One might take a car, another might take a plane, and another might take a ship to reach God. God is not different, only the vehicle to get there is different. So as the vehicle is different so is the terrain crossed.

Hinduism is ultimately a great synthesizer and none does this better than the great master Sri Aurobindo. In his approach he synthesizes East and West and in doing so reconciles the spiritual and the physical and finds the same, as everything is, as Brahman. As you have an evolution of the body, so also is there an evolution of the spirit and contrariwise.

The most interesting thing I find in Sri Aurobindo and I'm sure Aurobindo scholars would concur, is that you don't need to escape rebirth to become fully enlightened. You can become enlightened in the world in your physical body. This is similar to Buddhist teachings. No longer do you have to escape the body in a deep meditative state, and are only truly free when you escape the body, but rather you can be fully human and fully conscious at the same time. It reminds me of Hegel's book <u>The Phenomenology of Spirit</u> where he follows the dialectical transition in the unfolding of history. In other words there is a logic that is part of history which results in greater and greater understanding, and this too seems to be a sort of evolution of consciousness throughout humankind. But in order to have spirit there must be a manifestation in a body.

Without physicality how could we measure change? So the spirit is dependent on the body to manifest and ultimately is the body. Understanding this makes it clear that we can have our cake

15

and eat it to. We can become both spirit and body now. We can be enlightened in the body and this actually seems to be our assignment from God or Brahman. Being part of the human conditions in the world explains a part of the infinite possibilities of Brahman and helps establish the duality of existence and force, like a fires flame and its warmth.

One needs to look at the grand synthesis. This includes, for example, a synthesis of the world's religions; synthesis of mind/body, matter and spirit, also past, present and future, sleep and waking, division and unity; of the individual the cosmic and the transcendent; materialism and idealism, East and West and so on and so on. When one understands a synthesis, then how can it be the property of a world's particular people, rather it is universal.

When the unity of all things can be understood, then nothing can shake it. It reminds me of a quotation from the Tao Te Ching that "that which is firmly established is not easily uprooted." This unity is to be the strength of the Yoga Party.

Philosophy is not religion, in spite of what some people think; it is a way of understanding concepts, including the Ultimate Reality (Brahman). Brahman can not be known except through direct experience, but achieving a unity in all things results in a greater consciousness of Being and this helps one to realize their true interests, which is the interest of all. Perhaps achieving complete understanding results in pure insight.

The spirit is not the medieval entity that is released when one dies. It is rather something else and in fact according to Sri Aurobindo all is spirit, even matter, and also matter is spirit – neither having the upper hand. So how could this understanding of spirit be religious? Sri Aurobindo denied that his teachings were religion at all but rather spiritual. Understanding spirit one can understand the unity.

16

Integral Synthesis and the World's Religions

According to Vedanta all religion can be found within its framework. This idea is included in the Yogic tradition. All religion springs from the same source, which according to Vedanta is called Brahman. Other religions may call it something else, but essentially when one examines the possibilities of Brahman, which are infinite, it is easy to understand how in infinite possibilities, the many truths in religions follow only naturally at least on a conceptual basis. Like Vedantics, those of the Abrahamic traditions would undoubtedly agree that all things are possible with God.

The similarities surrounding religions are better understood when you understand the nature of Being. This is something that is attempted, perhaps not so successfully, in Jnana Yoga (intelligent inquiry). Being conceptually trained, it is natural that I emphasize this, although others may be differently inclined following other yogic paths. Understanding a synthesis of the eastern religions may seem easier than western religion, because it can usually be approached as simply an academic study. Similarities and differences can be identified with the reason for these differences, and how these differences can be reconciled from the Vedantic perspective.

Even more important is that the believers in these eastern historical traditions (excluding Islam) don't out of hand deny other belief systems generally or at least they don't claim all others are false and only theirs is truth. This is not true in the Abrahamic traditions. For example there is the case in Afghanistan of the man who converted to Christianity and according to the prevailing attitude in Afghanistan about apostasy, many clerics wanted him executed and at the very least severely punished.

17

In the Christian and Muslim traditions there is the attitude that other religions are somehow flawed, and in the Christian tradition especially other beliefs are not only flawed but dead wrong, and in some cases while you might not be punished in this life you are sentenced to an eternity of damnation. So a synthesis of the Abrahamic religions (e.g., Judaism, Christianity, and Islam) is especially problematic. Not because they cannot be reconciled efforts have been made in the Vedantic tradition that is thought of as adequate at least from their perspective. The larger problem for The Yoga Party is that while theoretically at least a synthesis can be arrived at, such a synthesis in the West is looked on as at the very least blasphemy and one only has to look at the history of war between the different Abrahamic schools to understand how this is such an important fact.

So The Yoga Party must tread lightly and once again reassure all member of whatever religious stripe that The Yoga Party is not religion, at least according to Aurobindo, but is rather spiritual, so it is hoped that this problem can be surmounted. Philosophy certainly is not based on faith and an integral understanding of the different religious schools is not essential to belief. In religion, at least in the Abrahamic tradition, it is belief that is important and nothing else. So let's start talking about the different religions and how they can be understood from a conceptual standpoint. This is based on understanding and not on belief. No claim is made here that understanding is superior to belief. Traditionally in the West, philosophy has been the "handmaiden" of religion in medieval times and this was nothing essential to the religious doctrine itself except as a scaffolding of support. So if these conceptual presuppositions can be synthesized it's all the better.

The Great Trinitarian Wisdom Traditions

Plato was undoubtedly the most influential philosopher in the West, with the possible exception of Aristotle which was Plato's student. The famous philosopher Whitehead said something to the effect that western thought is a footnote to Plato.

Philosophy is thought of as simply a way of thinking, and from Socrates the philosopher thought was based on a dialectical method where things were true based on argument and not on experiential considerations. These arguments were proofs, in many cases deductive proofs, which if you accepted the premises then the conclusions followed necessarily. In a nutshell this was the Socratic Method.

It's interesting to note that Socrates was one of the first philosophers that talked about social and political issues and this ultimately cost him his life. Philosophy before Socrates fell into largely the domain of natural science, predicting eclipses, forming hypotheses about what is essential matter, etc.

Yet an important fact to understand is that Plato accepted tenets of the Pythagorean School. We all know Pythagoras in science, well I'm sure most anyways. It is he or his followers that discovered the strange facts of the triangle, the idea that $c2 = a2 + b2$. This fact was to revolutionize science and is certainly fundamental (so I've heard) to higher mathematics. This is one of the important discoveries that have shaped western science and its prodigy technology.

The interesting thing about the Pythagorean cult is that it was a religious or perhaps spiritual mystical cult. It believed that the discoveries, including the facts surrounding triangles, showed us the mystical underpinnings of the natural, and told us something very phenomenal about its reality. In this sense it was metaphysical in a religious or perhaps spiritual sense. It is interesting that one

19

foundation of modern science is largely based on the teachings of a mystical cult.

It's no accident that science blossomed out of a religious tradition (e.g., Judeo-Christianity) that was based on a metaphysical duality between the supernatural and the natural world. Out of this comes the secularist attempt made by Descartes to reconcile the mind and body, this setting the stage for the objectivity of science and subsequently the scientific method.

While the proto-philosophers preceding Socrates were largely natural scientists, Plato, the neo-Pythagorean, added an element of the metaphysical and the ethical which was picked up later by the great philosopher Aristotle which formed the basis of knowledge for many hundreds of years.

But even more interesting than this fact I think is that many of the world's great wisdom traditions are based on these Trinitarian perspectives. I've often thought too that the great pyramids that are found around the world are linked to a cult emphasizing the great world Trinitarian tradition, being formed outwardly of an intricate construction of triangles all of which have three sides.

While most in the West are probably not convinced by this presentation, consider many of the world's great religious and spiritual traditions. In the West from Plato on we have a conceptual foundation for a metaphysical system, a scientific like inquiry and a system of ethics. This in some ways evolved into a dynamic religious system – within Christianity the Father, the Son and the Holy Ghost. The Father represents the metaphysical, while the Holy Ghost the inspiration of vitality in the natural universe, and the Son Christ, the great ethical and spiritual leader. In the synthesis of Christ all is thought to be contained in the trinity. This profound truth is awe inspiring but not only for the reasons some may suspect.

When one considers many of the major religious and spiritual wisdom traditions, one finds that they all carry a common thread.

Like Christianities' Father, Son and Holy Ghost, Vedanta has the idea of Brahman; that is the one referred to as Nirguna Brahman, which is understood as the dynamis of a trinity in the pantheon of Hindu cosmogony; first of Saguna Brahman – a personal God, second a sort of pantheism of the natural universe and lastly the individual Atman (e.g., the true self).

Modern Buddhism is largely a sect of Hinduism. It embraces many of Hinduism's tenets including reincarnation and karma. Yet Buddhism eschews metaphysics because of the excesses of the Brahmans, not unlike the Lutherans rejecting the excesses of the Catholic Church. In doing this, Buddhism, while not explicitly rejecting metaphysics, finds it unimportant, the only thing being important is the here and now. And in fact in a respect Buddhism negates Hinduism, rather like Marx inverts the idealism of Hegel and makes it material; the Buddha claims that the ultimate reality, for lack of better terminology, is a "Void." Yet Buddhism is little different from Hinduism because, as Hegel says, pure being is little different if at all from pure nothingness. Both are indescribable and unknowable.

Buddhism too talks about ethics, which is the one of the great contributions of the Siddhartha Gautama. Buddhism also talks about dependent origination which is the idea that nothing is essential and that everything exists only because everything else exists in the world. It is this concept which helps reconcile with the ultimate void.

Another important eastern tradition is Taoism where you have the dynamic Tao (Non-Being), the formless, which is a super structure of pure potentiality which results in the natural universe (Being). Out of these ideas comes Wu Wei, or to act in a natural manner, which forms the basis for an ethical system. For example one avoids unnecessary action except when action is natural. One would not act violently except when it was called for in perhaps

21

self defense or to protect other innocents. Out of this come the martial arts such as the Tai Chi Chuan which is considered to be an earthly manifestation of the Tao, and this natural aspect is found in the martial art forms that originated in the Shaolin temples or in the Japanese Zen monasteries. Zen is famous for pure awakening and living in the moment and there are famous stories of the excellence of Buddhist swordsman and archers based on this principle. This is ultimately individual action.

This is all for now about the trinity of the world wisdom traditions.

<u>The Unity of Peace and Joy</u>

When contrasting the eastern with western thought, one can begin to understand the reason for the differences between cultures. The Abrahamic religions rely on monotheism in which God is transcendent and the world is immanent. Only through Jesus, is the Father, Son and the Holy Spirit united according to the Christian tradition. This God Man reconciles the three manifestations of the transcendent, the universal, and the individual in a very particular way. This is one reason that Christians claim that their religion is the only truth and all others are heresy. This is what makes Jesus especially sacred and why only through Him you can know God.

This is very different from the eastern traditions. There is no locus or center from the ultimate viewpoint. All the traditions are ultimately homogeneous and rely on no discrete theistic understanding of God. This is true for Hinduism, Buddhism and Taoism. In Hinduism all is Brahman. In Buddhism the ultimate reality is unimportant and exists as a sort of metaphor as "the void." In Taoism we have this homogeneous like structure as well of the Tao, that is Non-being. Here too this non-being is primordial, but different in that a homeostatic relationship exists between non-being, being and ethics. This is the idea of the Chinese term for "The Mandate of Heaven" which says when the world is in order the king has the mandate of heaven and all is in accord. Here we have a sort of synthesis as well.

One may wonder if the Yoga Party is simply going to be a dispensation of my spiritual point of view. I think it is relevant because as John Lennon said rather than violence one should change one's mind instead. The mind is the source of violence and discord. Understanding the nature of the mind and its correlate,

Being, one can truly become transformed and contribute to a better world through a higher consciousness.

__The Locus of Life__

All things are equal in worth but saying that one must recognize that right away we are making a value judgment. To talk about worth at all one must assign some import, something not contained in the thing being bestowed this prize.

One thing we can say for sure is things are. Well maybe. Let say for now that the Buddha is wrong, or our understanding of the Buddha is wrong (lets take the second – it's more palatable) that that which is essential is not the Buddhist void. Let's say that things are.

So things are divided up into matter and space. Out of matter and space comes time, time being a measurement of change. Of course without matter and space no time could exist. With matter and no space time could not exist, and also with only space and no matter time could not exist. There would not be any condition for change. So suffice it to say that space and matter are necessary and sufficient conditions for time.

Thus comes change. Evolution is change. The path to a greater spiritual understanding is change. All results from change and this is all dependent on existence both physical and spiritual. Evolution is change over time in matter, and an enlarging God consciousness. Time is not a construct of Brahman, but rather time is the result of the infinite possibilities of Brahman and this includes matter and spirit. In fact matter and space, even regardless of time, both are necessary for life. An disembodied spirit cannot evolve and neither can a body, without life. Spirit is all. But existence is dependent on these individual types of spirit which enable Brahman to be all conscient rather than being inert. This comes about by "identity" as well as an amorphous Being.

So life is necessary. In order for evolution of the body or spirit, this identity of Being must exist. While the possible consciousness of humankind is unique and unlimited, it is uncertain to me that it is the locus of the identity of Being. I consider spirit to be the locus of Being and not humankind in itself.

It seems to me that vanity is the result of us seeing ourselves as central. First we were the only things with souls at the center of the universe, now we are supposedly the only species that has this ability to reason. This has resulted in the creation of many things. This creative capacity of humankind has taken on a sort of arrogance by people saying they are Gods. As Isaac Asimov once said, scientists are the new Gods.

It's not that I have a problem with humans being God. In fact I've said humans are God (Atman). But it's the type of God they see. Like their theistic heritage, they see themselves as a sort of transcendent, all knowing apotheosis of God. The Christian God has always smacked of anthropomorphism, but it seems now that the reverse is taking hold. This scientistic position is troublesome, mainly because it justifies all sorts of mischief because of their selfish understanding of their own virtues. This too stems from the idea that humans are the caretakers of the world as it says in the bible and take it to new lengths. Scientism a secular religion based on the Pythagorean mystics and today not so different from the perfection on earth espoused by Karl Marx, but with an emphasis on control and efficiency that only technology can provide.

Nevertheless humans always have considered themselves to be the locus of life and so it seem they will in the future. I'm not going to lecture here about the environmental degradation that has occurred due to scientism, but it's ironic that scientists clamor the most about global warming when they made the internal combustion engine, just as we fear the consequences of nuclear war while we praise the mathematical formulations of the great physicist Einstein. I'm resigned to the growth of the human population and the continuing degradation for the earth's species;

26

and scientism, while not the root of the problem, carries on this tradition of human self-centeredness.

Our great brains. Those beacons of light. The thing most prized in society is the ability to get machines think like us and in fact go beyond us, such is the valuing of intellect. I won't talk at this time about the result of this spread of technology, but it seems to be rooted in the idea of an objectified self in a box. Technology in one's own image. By objectifying oneself one tries to find value.

Yet all claim that that it is our brains that make us so superior (a value judgment) and therefore we are entitled to all kinds of privileges. I told one of my classes once that if instead we valued speed rather than brains, we would consider the cheetah as the most advanced animal. One of my students responded, "yeah but we could just shoot it!" Such is the sad state of affairs of the human specie.

All life has value, all life shares in the spirit. It seems to be claimed by the master Aurobindo that humans are more conscious and more "evolved" being able to come to a greater realization of Brahman. I must differ with this. I think this contributes to the worldview of the centrality of the human being and in some respects can be used as a justification for the subjugation of other species.

Certainly Brahman doesn't have a preference, at least in the sense that all is Brahman and all life is spirit. Who is to say the evolution of humans is superior (a value judgment) to the evolution of plants or algae. All things are sacred and are the product of divine creation. Here the Buddha is certainly most correct as I understand ahimsa. The sacredness and therefore the value of all (a moral judgment) must say that we are all evolving.

The trees produce the air, the plants and animals supply our food (well not animals if you are vegetarian) and often our medicine. Evolution is the evolution of all. We are part and parcel;

27

past, present and future of this heritage of divine Being. Nothing should be ignored or marginalized and nothing is superior.

Protect life. The spirit cares nothing what form it be just acting out the change of existence in identity. Through being enlightened beings we can enjoy the fruits of the beauty of Brahman rather than be destroyed in some vain despair.

Pleasure, Joy and the Inspiration of Writing

According to the Master Aurobindo, life seems painful but in fact when you achieve God Consciousness it is bliss. How could it be anything else being reunited with the divine.

The Buddha says "Life is Suffering." The path of the Buddha is to escape rebirth and therefore escape suffering. Suffering comes from identifying with the body. One might say, if I touch a hot stove I feel pain and God Consciousness will not prevent that pain. This certainly seems true, but I'm reminded of people walking across hot coals and feeling nothing, even as their feet smoke.

Socrates said that he had pleasure when the chains were removed from his ankles prior to his execution. It seems that pleasure and pain are hopelessly intertwined. One thing I have told my students is that one of the most pleasant experiences one can have is injecting heroin. I have some inkling of what that is like because once when I had an abdominal abscess they gave me a shot of morphine.

Like many of the things that cause pleasure with heroin an incremental increase of the drug is needed to achieve the same degree of pleasure. This is called tolerance. Ultimately, as with heroin, there is no pleasure at all with long term use and the only goal is to keep at bay the pain of withdrawal. Such is the nature of pleasure.

There is a basic difference between pleasure and joy. There is no pleasure when one achieves bliss in God Consciousness, just joy. Pleasure is the result of having a body and bliss is the product of divine consciousness which is a great joy. Writing inspires me.

The Evolution of Spirit

The Yoga Party emphasizes peace, compassion and insight. In addition the Yoga Party resists injustice. The Yoga Party is for a fair wage and meaningful work. All people are worthy of the same dignity. As well all life must be protected because all embody Brahman. In addition the physical structure of the world must not be destroyed, because this would result in the suffering of life.

Only through consciousness can one begin to appreciate life. If life is marginalized then consciousness cannot come about. Life is moving through an evolution of Being. When this life is destroyed then consciousness cannot accrue and it is lost.

Aurobindo's vision is a hopeful one. Since we are undergoing a physical as well as a spiritual evolution, this is the movement and flow of the spirit which occurs in the cosmos in a natural manner. The Yoga Party is confident that its goals can be achieved. Because evolution is the nature of things, then evil (separation from the divine) will be removed in short order.

But I must emphasize that if this experiment in evolution fails, then Brahman will not despair. Brahman is not an anthropomorphic God and transcends all conception. We can question about it through Jnana Yoga, but we cannot really see it except perhaps by direct experience. If the world is destroyed, then this is simply one manifestation of the infinite possibilities of Brahman. Nothing can be forced. Surely life will rise again and start over, if not here, then somewhere else if at all. Evolution continues.

But if we protect life and the planet to maintain a spiritual life, this would not be selfishness, because all would benefit and in the cosmos this would be a natural course.

All is Compassion - Compassion is All

All is compassion. Compassion is all. The machinations between individuals and between classes matter little when one has compassion. Compassion is the medicine that cures despair. False consciousness regarding one's own interests results in class jealousy and hatred.

There is no class. Classes are a form of false consciousness. There is ultimately no life or death; they are just the cosmic manifestations of Brahman in temporality. Little really matters except consciousness. There is no hatred in consciousness, no despair, no jealousy and no greed. What is is, and what is not will not or can not be, according to the manifestations of infinite Being in its own accord of limitation. Consciousness is teacher and lord.

Those that would leave the world behind to escape the wheel of illusion would be acting for "ones'" own benefit which of course indulges the illusion of "self."

Humans feel stress, feel hungry, and get tired. This is part of the human condition. But the bondage of self can be overcome, like mental infirmities that often strike a great genius. It is the bondage of our being that helps us, provides the impetus, to escape to God Consciousness. Thus is the evolution of spirit.

There is horror in the world. Disaster strikes all. One can become disillusioned and dismayed. But the aware, the conscious ones understand this is the human condition; their predicament, that can only come about by the dance of Being in infinity.

For identity, with the infinite that narrates the drama unfolding before us, one can escape the karma that binds us in the world and live in the state of divinity, ministering to all that suffer.

All is Compassion. Compassion is All.

The Quandary of Matter and Spirit

The mistake is often made to make a distinction between matter and spirit. In fact all is Brahman. While traditional Hinduism seems to make the claim that that which is real is spirit, in fact all is spirit both matter and spirit.

Descartes struggled to explain how the mind and body interact. It is an insoluble problem. The mind is atemporal and aspatial, the body temporal and spatial. So not only are the mind and body dissimilar, they are exact opposites. The western conception of the spirit comes from western medieval theology, where the "mind" is a sort of geist (ghost) which dwells in the material shell.

Descartes, as well as being a brilliant mathematician, was also a great philosopher. He set the foundation for science by inventing a skeptical system which would ostensibly remove all doubt. All of this is built around his cogito "I think, therefore I am." In other words out of the antecedent "thinking" comes the necessary (a priori) consequent existence. That which thinks must exist. But Descartes' claim was an epistemological (a theory about knowledge) rather than a metaphysical claim (understanding reality). While Descartes theory is useful as far as a model for skepticism about what we can "know," it says nothing about what can Be.

This is where Descartes theory comes apart. If we can't explain the relationship between mind and body we cannot explain the relationship between spirit and matter. Must the difference between the two be irreconcilable? The idea of the distinction between geist and worldly bodies is the result of a dogmatic system relying on a transcendent atemporal aspatial realm, and then the cosmos where matter lies. And never the twain shall meet. Yet according to western tradition this matter/spirit distinction explains life.

32

Aurobindo, unlike the traditional Hindu's, does not make a distinction between matter and spirit. Unlike the traditional Hindu's which says that identifying one as an individual body is illusion, in fact we are all Brahman, Aurobindo takes them a bit further and says that matter is not in fact an illusion and something to be transcended in spirit but rather that matter is spirit as all things are spirit. In other word matter is truly real from Aurobindo's perspective. This may not seem reasonable to the westerner but consider the following.

We claim to be free, capable of free choice. Free choice of course is indispensable, in for instance a democracy. If one were not in fact free then a democracy would mean nothing. This freedom seems to come about through the grace of God, God in the West being transcendent. By the same token we are physical, subject to the same physical, chemical, biological, environmental laws that govern all life. So how are we to reconcile freedom vs. determinism? This is really what Descartes is trying to do at least from a metaphysical standpoint. We are a free spirit that thinks freely; therefore we know we must exist in the world, as it seems as a physical body. So this argument of freedom, while not thrown out completely, does not seem to be supported by Descartes cogito. Because of the completely dissimilar mind/body duality to explain the thinking thing the cogito must be thrown out. But we don't throw the baby out with the bathwater so to speak.

An attempt has been made to say we are all material. That is we are the firing of neurotransmitters in the brain. There have even been studies that show the firing pattern in the brain "remembers" that pattern when a similar stimulus occurs again causing a similar pattern neuronal firing. This idea could be thought to explain thought, memory and insight depending on the depth of the neural connections. John Locke provides a philosophical system that seems to support this.

33

But a small problem cannot really be avoided if we think about it clearly. If there is no spirit, that is the thing that thinks freely, and in fact we are all physical bound by the different necessary forces in the cosmos, then how can we really say we have free thought at all? Perhaps I writing is just part of a necessary history which is forcing me to unfold. This is a rather bitter pill to swallow. Are there any other alternatives?

The all is matter quandary can be dealt with and perhaps resolved when one takes the perspective that all is spirit. This doesn't really seem to be nonsensical, at least from a physicalist perspective when you consider there is in fact a certain order that drives inert matter as well as life. At least on an atomic scale one comes to realize that all matter is energy. One only needs to look at Einstein's $E=mc2$. Do we really look at matter as pure energy? No! There is even an attempt to explain creation from a physicalist perspective.

Life seems to be inspirited, we act, we love, we procreate etc. But the lively swirling of atoms that compose our being is in the same state of motion in inert matter. It seems clear then at least at the atomic level, matter and energy is not really different.

If they are not really different, except perhaps composed of different atoms, although carbon exists in coal mines as well as human bodies, they really operate in the same manner. So what does that have to do with freedom? If matter is pure energy bound by the laws of physics then aren't we determined?

We still see things as things. This results from ignorance. According to Aurobindo; like nature, this seems to be evidence of physical change over time, so there is its corollary spirit which essentially is not different since all is spirit. They really are part and parcel of the same thing. The only reason we do not recognize matter as spirit is because of ignorance. This is where Vishnu, the preserver, sleeps.

34

Brahman in its dance of infinity seeks identity. Something without identity, like a subset without a master set, is amorphous and cannot be truly conscious. It is through the play of infinity that change comes about. It is through the play of infinity that, as Hegel said, it is the spirit coming to know itself. This is the advance of wisdom.

If anyone tells you Hinduism is simply transcendentalism, they are uninformed or are liars. Because of the nature of spirit no distinction can be made between the eternal Brahman, the cosmos and the individual with God within. The free play of the infinite creates freedom in spirit and gives the cosmos a central vital part in the evolution of life and spirit. We are not illusion, we are not a ghost within the machine, but are spirit (Brahman).

Since we understand the importance of spirit coming to know itself, we must practice action, but not action that destroys, maims, kills, tortures, murders etc. For we are the divine in spirit and in consciousness we can see our true calling in the world and that is to cultivate insight, have compassion, and find tranquility that preserves all things, both matter and spirit. Only then can evolution continue whether you are a Darwinist or a Hegelian, or an Indian mystic.

A Flower

This idea I acquired and have subsequently expanded on is from a Buddhist writing whose author I cannot recall as I wish I could in some way give credit. I hope they will forgive me for taking any license.

The different bases for knowledge are different depending on the field. Science tends to be very empirical, psychology analytical, sociology statistical and art inspirational and so on. Yet all is knowledge. How are we to decide that they all spring from the same source? The jargon is different, the skills used are disparate and the outcomes are variable. How can we understand this?

A flower. Let's take a flower. We can understand a flower scientifically as having a chemical, physical and botanical structure.

We can understand a flower as an essential part of an ecosystem.

We can understand the flower as a result of a primordial big bang.

We can think of the flower as a creation of God and revere it as such.

We can think of a flower as a source of food for some animals, as well as form of exquisite intoxication for the honey bee.

We can understand it as a form of the continuing evolution of life.

We can think of it as a source for medicines and herbal treatments.

The lotus sutra is a great Buddhist story about how the teaching of the Buddha was passed on to his disciple through the presentation of a lotus flower.

The lotus posture is a famous Buddhist posture for meditation.

We can also understand its beauty as being a source for art and in the act of giving showing love.

Let's take in particular the poppy. It can be used to produce opium which is a boon to medicine in pain control.

It can also be used economically by a state as it's primary export as in Afghanistan.

Further it can be synthesized into heroin which has caused the death and downfall due to addiction.

Not only has heroin and the drug trade resulted in many deaths, but is a primary ingredient in the financial integrity of many youth drug peddlers and dealers in the inner cities and results in crime and degeneracy.

It can also result, when injected, in a euphoria that is unmatched.

Drug addiction has resulted in people finding God (imagine that!) through 12 step programs and psychotherapy aimed at recovery.

Our prisons are filled with former addicts and dealers in supermaxx prisons living in their cells 23 hours a day. Perhaps half of all criminal justice employment and a major expense for taxpayers is a result of the criminalization of drug use. Political fortunes are made on prosecuting those guilty of violating drug laws.

Compulsive labor exists in the prisons which can and is used to break the back of alien corporations with a new slave caste.

Drug addiction destroys families.

The ideology of a war on everything, including war itself, is the war on drugs.

Historically a whole nation was enslaved by addiction by the commerce of the British in the opium drug trade, providing the opium product to the Chinese mainland with the goal of obtaining trade rights.

The use of shared needles has resulted in a tremendous spread of AIDS around the world, especially in the US.

Drug addiction is railed against in the churches as the result of moral degeneracy. And we could continue to go on and on.

Such is the nature of understanding a flower. But simply a flower is a flower. It has no intrinsic value in itself except as a manifestation of the universal spirit. It is valuable in any sense that it is useful to someone or something.

The many ways of investigating a flower then depend on what is trying to be accomplished. One reason we have so many ways of knowing it is because in the West we emphasize the compartmentalizing of knowledge into discrete fields. This ability has resulted in a great advance of knowledge, at the expense of understanding where different disciplinary fields overlap and how they overlap. Ultimately, in its essence, it is a simply a flower and exists as such, nothing more and nothing less. We can only understand it fully by understanding all that it is, not the sum of its characteristics but how it presents itself in its totality.

Consciousness is the key.

Brahman and the Transcendental and Cosmic Split

God determines the laws of the universe that is in Hinduism Brahma the creator. If the creation is infinite, then how can we talk about a transcendental/cosmic split?

So how is the cosmos limited and how is Brahman unlimited? Certainly the cosmos (the universe) has a natural set of laws. There are laws of thermodynamics and gravity. These laws are invariable.

It seems clear that without creation we would have nothing. As Lucretius said in a metaphor, infinity is when a spear is thrown and it just keeps on going on and on. If all was solidity then of course the spear wouldn't fly. Certainly this then would be something and finite or so it seems unless solidity was endless as well. And if there were nothing then the spear would fly and fly in nothingness. But is nothingness endless space? Do the laws of thermodynamics and gravity hold in empty endless space? This seems to be a contradiction.

The question really boils down to is empty space Being or not? When talking about the transcendental and the cosmic, we are asking is the transcendental pure Being and the cosmic not? In other words is the cosmic Maya (e.g., ignorance) illusion and the transcendental Brahman that which is truly real? Or is there spirit in nothingness that is the spirit of the cosmos? Certainly endless cosmic nothingness would have no time or space as we know it. Space and time could not exist without a frame of reference. Time measures change and what could change in infinite nothingness? We really couldn't talk about space either in this endless space. To talk about space within endless space we must have a frame of reference to know that space exists spatially.

So again I make the claim that matter and space are inexorably bound. An endless space, an endless void which would have as its contrary opposite endless solidity, must share the same qualities. No frame of reference, no space, no time. Would either be primordial? I think not.

At this point it should be clear that matter and space are a necessary condition for the play of Brahman coming to know itself. Without matter or without space nothing could change, no flux. There could be no alarm clock ringing in the morning. There could be no baby crying. The boss could not make unreasonable demands on your time. Existence is the fruit of Brahman. Without existence Brahman could not be truly infinite in actuality and in fact would be nothing. The infinite is capable of all things, and without both space and matter nothing could change, nothing could occur and at least in a sense, nothing could exist.

God and Mammon

Another day dawns around the world. People rise and scurry hastily to their jobs. None know of the others life; none know of the others cares. Only the self must survive, and to survive one must work to live.

Scurrying about doing what has to be done we have become cogs in the machine; cogs in the machine of capitalism. Grinding, forever grinding, and hoping our limbs and our life don't get crushed by the turning wheels.

Days pass on. One day into the other. Life drifts by and by and then it is time to die. Do we know where we came from? Do we know where we are going?

As the great master Hegel mused, the master drives the slave. The slave serves the master. The master feeds off the slave like a parasite, living off their toil. Is this unfair? I think not. The master learns nothing new, and if the master did know something before they forget. And if the slave knew nothing to begin with through their toil to stay alive they learn much. They learn how to live. One day the slave becomes the master of the master and the master becomes the slave to the slave.

This is because the slave, in doing what it must to preserve its life, loses their fear of death as life becomes hell on earth. This is why the slave who was afraid may rise up against the master fearless. And why does the master become fearful after long subjecting the slave?

The master lives a life void of meaning. Their rings, their palaces, their fine wine, their love conquests, their horses and their polo and their crown and their kingdoms come to mean nothing. So they think they need more. If they have more, so they think, then maybe they can overcome this wretched boredom that irks them like an itch that a scratch cannot soothe.

42

While the slave knows what their life is, a life of drudgery, the master knows not what their life is at all. Pleasure, success, power is the drug that drives them. In order to love themselves they idealize themselves and their own imagined prowess as they wage wars, practice genocide and drive the slaves. They rationalize their dominance because otherwise they couldn't live on as they are.

And being possessed of so much power and success and gold and gems, before they die they cry out loud. This is mine, this is mine! And then they die. Their loss is great.

The slave on the other hand looks to the world beyond. Believing in a blissful afterlife helps them survive their day to day struggle. When they die it is a release from the sacrifice made to the master, which they do out of humility and service to God. In their often short lives they cry out in devotion to their loving God and they kiss the feet of its holy icons...

Neither rich nor poor recognize their own interests!

The rich think to live long and prosper, lost in the dreamy reveries of conquest and courage that they will never die. The poor have the advantage of not fearing death and looking forward to being reunited with God.

But when they both die they are reunited in spirit. In fact they were never different, just living out the dream of Vishnu the preserver, both tied to their soul as individuals in the material world. While the slave knows the creator the rich may not. If the slave dies a slave they have lived a fuller life because they have tasted life and they have learned the lesson of matter and spirit and have grown in courage and strength.

But during their lives when the slave loses fear of death altogether, then the master cannot impose their will. The transition of the master/slave dialectic is a dynamic that is played out in the dance of primordial creation. In this dance the slave becomes the master, and the master becomes the slave, and then this dance can begin again.

43

Where does the spiritual evolution come about that Aurobindo believes leads us to a greater consciousness? If the slave continues to rise up to slay and enslave the master then the new slave begins to learn again. Meanwhile the dreams of conquest and power driven by greed and jealousy and revenge with the adornments of gold and jewels, and fiefdoms and kingdoms and crowns are reborn anew. Like someone digging a ditch and then filling it in again is anything accomplished?

The ruling class will always decay and the slave class will always revolt as time is on their side.

Such is the play of life in class systems, riches piling up and then tumbling down only to rise again.

But who stands on the mountain? Who dwells in the valley? As the mountain depends on a valley to stand tall, so does a valley depend on the great peaks to find its place lovingly close to the earth. And as the storms and earthquakes and glaciers wear away at the mountains other mountains climb up and other valleys are burrowed out.

Whirling and twirling around the sun, through the galaxy, expanding ever so quickly from the centerless center perhaps forever to end in cold dispersion or to return to the vortex of the primordial storm only to roar outward in its infinite fire once again.

But our small blue and yellow planet for now persists. We live our lives not knowing what or why. We are a very small part and at the same time a very core component of all that drives being as Being drives all.

The rings of God the eternal, God the creator, God the universe and God the person, gives of itself always, whether in loving kindness on earth or in the bliss of union. If the light of consciousness does not shine now then perhaps later, and if not then, later still.

But the chance is there. We can know and also be God. Or we can be both the salt of the earth and can also be mammon. The

44

spirit drives on and one day the flame of insight will flicker and with its warmth and light it will begin to shine, and the world, like life under the flaming sun will grow and all will climb up on the precipice and see the distant valley and world and worlds to come. The day will come. It has to come. For if it doesn't come then what is life?

Life cannot be a fallow land. Things grow and thrive and strive to survive and change to be what they can be God permitting. Just as life and spirit finds a way so will God. For if not God would die. Nietzsche said God is dead. God did not die because God was mortal, but because God no longer mattered to life and life mattered nothing to itself. Yet God lives whether people see God or not. To reach God one must reach out or inward in oneself. To find God one must search. To find God in your heart you must feel. To live forever you must find your own true self, this spiritual essence. Only then can we survive this world together.

Secular Religion

Science is mystical and recondite. It is mystical in that mathematical calculations not only approximate reality, but in fact as Einstein said it is reality.

Cosmology used to fall into the discipline of Philosophy. It was only "natural" that science took this task over as it has turned out to have more useful tools than Philosophy.

The interesting thing to note is that the Pythagorean Theorem, posited by Pythagoras' tribe, was based on a mystical belief system, not unlike what Einstein believed about math and reality. The Pythagorean Theorem is central in Trigonometry and Calculus, and so is fundamental for understanding gravity and thermodynamics.

Yet this foundational innovation (e.g., the Pythagorean Theorem) is now based on the belief that somehow mathematics was the only thing that could explain the cosmos and in fact all things are determined by the Holy Integer. It's no accident that the title of one of Hawking's books is called "God Created the Integers." We now have the alpha and beta. There is a leap of faith to accept the fact that somehow mathematics is what is real in the universe. Once again this idea fits in with a supernatural creator.

Plato was a neo-Pythagorean that used the Pythagorean ineffable belief system to explain the Platonic forms, which had a great deal of influence on later Christianity.

Maybe you are still not convinced. There is a simple problem. If mathematics is what the world is, then we are determined. And if mathematics only describes the world, then how can we know it really describes anything at all?

We have a long history of Ptolemy, Copernicus, Euclid, and Newton whose systems had fundamental flaws, or at least were not complete solutions, but only approximated what is now considered truth. Now Einstein has the final word, or so it seems. But as we have found out, Quantum Mechanics has been a perennial thorn in his side. So which is it, reality or description? Neither seems to work, at least so far.

It should be amply clear why it is recondite. People, in their attempt to create more exacting mathematical systems, have left the past behind. So those that create original innovation only know their own system, at least till others can be taught. So in this sense science is like an elite aristocracy, whose kings are always subject to being deposed.

It's seems the dichotomy has been somewhat resolved. The scientists are the new priests; just look at the expert in chemistry, physics, mathematics and biology, the medical doctor in their white coats. As with the cosmologist, the applied physicist, considered to be our greatest thinker, we have adopted based largely on authority, technocracy, embodied in the shell of capitalism, which is like a car that runs without a driver.

This prizing of technology, as a manifestation of what is real and also authoritatively based on mathematical principles, makes it that which determines our existence, which ultimately is of a force that drives itself and in doing so drives us all.

This is what I mean by secular religion.

There is an Intrinsic Equality of All in the World

One problem I have with Hinduism in general and Sri Aurobindo in particular, is the idea that humans are supreme because of consciousness. This is where I depart from classical Indian thought.

Such ideas result in a sort of anthropocentrism (human centered) view of life which results in placing regard the highest, and perhaps only, on the human specie. This is very unfortunate because with this emphasis there can and does come a callous disregard for all other forms of life.

A similar situation is found in Christianity where only the human is inspirited and all over living things are simply animistic (animals). This too can lead to a sort of disregard that results in a sort of callousness to other forms of life, although it can be claimed, and I think it is true, that such an attitude is not a necessary consequence, all being the creation of God. In this respect then one can take the position that while all life is not inspired, all is the result of God's creation and therefore in a sense all if holy.

This is very different from the criticism based on the interpretation from Genesis that all that exists in God's creation is for the use of inspired beings (humans). This can and does result in a callous disregard for things other than humans including plants, animals, and things of beauty in nature such as rock formations and glaciers and the like.

On the other hand if the interpretation is taken that we are caretakers or conscientious stewards of the world and respect it as God's creation, then care and nourishing of all that exists becomes possible and even likely. Unfortunately the ambiguousness in this regard regarding stewardship as opposed to use results in very different attitude regarding all that exists.

This problem does not seem to exist in Hinduism. All is Brahman or the One. All are spirit. While creation is a part of Hinduism, being an action of Brahma in the creation of the Cosmos, this manifestation of Being is subsumed under the idea of Brahman as being the indescribable, that which either acts of not, is dynamic or static. This does not then give the impetus for the creation of all as being foundational and therefore divine, except that all is divine and therefore truly undifferentiated in the amorphous mass of infinite possibilities.

Yet Hinduism is most certainly anthropocentric. The life of one is unmasking the God within us and rising to a greater consciousness by experiencing the God within. Humans are considered to be the most advanced because they have this enlarged capacity for consciousness. All living things must pass through the human form to escape rebirth and finally eliminate karma and be reunited with God in ones consciousness. This reminds me of the narrower sense in the evolution of consciousness made by the Brahmin (priestly) caste that the Buddha railed against as requiring a sort of indulgence in order to be holy and escape rebirth.

In this metaphor then the animals are the merchant castes, the plants are the workers and the physicality of the world is composed of the untouchables. Of course looking at it this way is untenable and must be rejected. It seems clear; to me at least, the result of looking at things from the anthropocentric perspective potentially can be more harmful to the integrity of all that exists than the previously stated Christian interpretation regarding use or its other interpretation, stewardship of the world.

So what are we to do? Do we need to throw Hinduism out? What is the solution? What we need is a new basis for value. If all is Brahman then there is no essential hierarchy in life. While it may or may not be true that humans are more capable of a meaningful consciousness that other life forms, one wonders if this is even important in the scheme of things. Something certainly seems skewed here if this highest form of consciousness does not find a necessity for preserving all the manifestations of Brahman.

Since all things are inspirited in Hinduism or at least according to Sri Aurobindo, it would at least be thought that all things have equal value. It is doubtful that God has any preference and of course in Hinduism God does not.

But what is one to do with the idea of spiritual evolution and the requirement of God knowing itself and deriving it action from this identification, and this fact being instrumental in a human consciousness.

But since all things are joined ultimately, then certainly as a value, the care of all must be protected. A consciousness that does not do this in the least is most certainly flawed and even sinister. So at least in the Hindu scheme of things all must flourish without any sacrificial lambs made by the human God conscious being. To do less contradicts the nature of Brahman.

But what then are we to value? The answer is to value all. Always, independent of our supposed spiritual progress, all that exists, is foundational and ultimately constitutionally all that is all. To discriminate based on consciousness clearly seems a mistake. The human being is like a Goliath standing on the shoulders of even greater giants. The connection cannot be overlooked nor can it be lost.

All then must be valued equally. Consciousness is not a quality that justifies any action that is not in harmony with the world that sustains us. All must be cared for. All must flourish under human care. This is a necessary pre-condition and proscription if one is to take the position that human consciousness is important at all.

There is an intrinsic equality of all in the world.

50

The Golden Butterfly of Liberty

Is freedom important?

What is freedom?

Freedom is an inalienable right. What does this mean? It means that a government cannot bestow or take away freedom from its people. Freedom is God given, something that we should and hopefully do cherish. But what are the roots of freedom?

Freedom is based largely on our Judeo-Christian tradition. We being God's children are able to know right from wrong and to act accordingly. People who are not free cannot be responsible for their actions, for to commit a wrong act one must decide to commit this act freely. Right or wrong, what we do defines ourselves and gives us our individual and group character. Unfortunately in the Christian tradition we are thought to have fallen from grace and therefore be sinful in nature. What implications does this have?

If people are sinful in nature then men and/or women must be protected from each other. Society must be protected too from its people. People must be punished for their evil behavior. Spare the rod spoil the child, while not in vogue, still determines our criminal justice system. People for petty crimes are locked up to "protect society" from their supposed heinous acts. Crimes of moral turpitude are especially frowned upon especially if committed by one that has fallen from favor in the eyes of God – the poor.

The poor, having fallen from favor in God's eyes, are especially suspect and comprise the vast majority of our prisons and are compelled to do forced labor. On the other hand, those more favored – the rich, are punished less severely, they are the beautiful

51

people, those that we look up to and idolize simply because of their wealth.

Now this threat of terrorism. We live in a state of fear, the state fears losing its power and acts on the pretense that they are protecting the people.

What good is a life without freedom? As Thomas Jefferson said, if you give up freedom for security you have neither. Do we want to live in a state run by tyranny? Thomas Paine said give me liberty or give me death. Oh Tom where have you gone?

Where are all the freedom loving people? Where have you gone? Those thankful sang of liberty that they loved so well. You people of standards and values declaring your love for the land you love so well because you can stand free! Where have you gone? Oh where.

And the religious right supports these actions as a way to stamp out the evil terrorists who worship a pagan god. Because of the shedding of the blood of Jesus, none must tread on our path – and we will not be detained on our way, nor allow those to block our way in the steady march of God's dominion. How did these people become so blind?

Like Judaism, Christianity is a religion based on suffering and slavery. Surely the Christians don't think that simply because they are on top, that what they do is right even though they may be betraying the very principles, the principles of freedom, which they so ardently profess? Even if it is right who might be next? Are you Christians the government or a tool of the government? Do you really want to find out?

From the slavery out of Egypt, to the crucifixion of Christ and from throwing the Christians to the lions in ancient Rome, but also the burning of the library in Alexandria, the Spanish Inquisition and the Crusades, all revolve around the central idea of freedom, something that we should not easily discard. Where is the valuing of freedom now?

Have you given up on the freedom given to you by your loving God? Do you not trust in his judgment? From whatever measure you take will be measured tenfold on you. Where are you leading us dear Christians? Are you building the prison that will house you? Are you building the walls that will divide you? Are you giving up your divine rights to a divine king? What happened to you and what is happening to your rights?

Is freedom necessary in the grand scheme of things? Do I for instance care about freedom at all? Well I must say I do. As a child every day in school I stood up and said the pledge of allegiance to say "with freedom and justice for all." I have also at times raised my hand up and sworn to preserve, protect and defend the constitution. Do I take these things seriously? I must say yes.

While I was compelled to do this by the government (ironic isn't it) I am loyal to my government and in spite of my criticism I am very proud to be an American and I love my country. If I didn't speak out again injustice what a grievous fault that would be.

It doesn't matter a whit to universal Being whether I am enslaved or free. All is the unfolding of Being coming to know itself. It acts freely except through its own constraints and like Shakespeare's plays all are actors in this great dream of Vishnu.

But I have a role to play and I take my role very seriously. I am here now. And I am here because I am the dynamic manifestation of Being coming to know itself and that for me is freedom. There is no consciousness without freedom. There is no love. There is no hope. There is no compassion. There is only evil and those that purvey it.

So freedom is gone or it is flying away like a butterfly on golden wings. Oh beautiful butterfly, why must you go? Why must your stay be so short? Why must you leave me here? Go ahead then and flitter away – Goodbye.

The New School of Consciousness Only

What is consciousness?

We understand consciousness as beings having awareness. We are aware of our surroundings. We are sentient beings who can perceive the "real world".

But is the world as we perceive it the way that it exists in itself? It seems not. If someone is colorblind lets say to bright red and green then they see things as greater or lesser shades of grey, unlike the one with normal color vision.

Or for example take the vision of a fly and the vision of human. Since the structure of the eye is so different then the nature of the vision is also very different.

The way something sees suits the organism as it exists in the world.

Who is to say that a human perception is superior to a fly's vision? Each serves it's individual needs, for if it did not it would change or perish. Certainly something so transient cannot represent the infinite eternal except as a manifestations of it myriad potentials. Something so transitory cannot manifest the eternal.

How can we understand the limitations of the sentience? How can we understand what the transient sentient thing understands about the infinite nature?

Likewise we understand ourselves as passing through time. We are born, age and die. We understand time through change. If there is no change then doubtless there could be no time, as change is what is truly real and not time according to Einstein.

If we dwell in the infinite as finite things then how can we exist at all? How can a thing in itself be part of something that has no limit?

First of all we need to understand the nature of consciousness in time. All things are possible so there are no limits on how physical and therefore psychical conditions can be. There is no speed to time or limits on time because in fact time does not exist only but as change whose possibilities are limitless.

How do we understand time in our egoistic consciousness? We cannot perceive the nature of egoistic perception, first of all because they ego is just a way of the universal spirit to come and know itself and to do that it must be limited in itself. Strictly we are Being coming to know itself. Nothing can have identity without some sort of self-recognition. If that which perceives and which is perceived are identical then no identity has been arrived at. So at least from a logical perspective the ego must be somehow limited in its understanding.

Our limited understanding of time as the changes that occur outside as well as the aging of the body points to a linear way of understanding ourselves and the world, although it is possible to not be so linear in other cultures. Once again like sentience, the way we understand time depends on the structure of the ego. This varies from culture to culture. As ego consciousness varies from culture to culture and individual to individual, so does the God consciousness differ from ego consciousness in a like manner.

While we think of time as measuring change, time itself is immeasurable. Before the change begins it ends. We cannot find the time to be, for to find it it only has disappeared into something else which is not. There is no present for once we apprehend it it is gone. If there is no present then there is no future nor past. Infinite being does not rely on this limitation of past, present and future.

So what is this place where things are centered? It is like the nature of a triangle. It is an invention of the ego that describes the nature of reality. Of course no triangles exist, for a triangle is a figure that has no depth, composed of lines that have no width nor depth, composed of points which have no length or width nor depth. It seems safe to say that triangles then do not really exist except in our minds. Yet ideas are a way of ordering our world and such is the practical use of time.

So when we see this divisor between past and future we are talking about something that does not really exist but is only a product of the egoistic understanding. A point in time is like a point in a line, it has no temporal or spatial qualities just as the infinite does not possess these.

As centered as that point in time the present is; it is not surprising because our egoistic consciousness stuck in this present superimposed on the infinity of God or Brahman is understood by the ego as a empty point, something that can only be experienced through consciousness but cannot really be understood or described.

What else would we expect from something that is misunderstood as being in time in a timeless realm, as finite infinity? Something recognized as being finite with the infinite as its base must be like our pointless point, a form of blindness for the egoistic consciousness. How else could the infinite be understood by the ignorance of the egoistic consciousness rather than being something strictly in the moment?

As beings in the world then we live seemingly from moment to moment. We live in the moment. Our being coming to know the infinite Being requires this. How indeed could this be otherwise? Being in the moment is divine consciousness.

This is what I call the new school of consciousness only.

The Identity of God

How can we understand the identity of God? What do we mean by the identity of God? Why is the identity of God important?

First of all we must discuss what we mean by God. What is God? When we talk about God we must be careful not to anthropomorphize God. God does not have a sex, is not big and tall (or short and little for that matter). God does not cogitate. God does not eat or sleep nor does God excrete.

Anthropomorphic ways of understanding God are useful for those that only understand the physical world. It is a way of grasping the eternal by using what is most familiar. While this may be pacifying to one this does little toward divine consciousness.

Granted when I talk about God I am talking about infinite Being. In a sense God can be thought to be like humans. For example God creates and God destroys – and in turns God nourishes life and God destroys life. God creates the seasons of the year with the springing forth of life in the spring and the decay in the fall.

But these qualities are not what God is in its essence. This is because God is infinite. How could God have qualities in its essence if it is finite? It doesn't seem to me at least that such a thing could be possible.

Yet if God is a sort of amorphous mass, how can we explain existence and creation at all? What would be the original cause of God? What would cause the infinite to manifest itself in the myriad existence?

Once again it is important to note that if God can be both essence and existence, in a sense both potential and manifestation, then in fact we are all God, not Gods. We all spring from the same source. All things spring from the same source as well. Ultimately we cannot draw a distinction between matter and what some call spirit. Understanding this one can overcome the perennial problem of matter and consciousness as typified in Descartes Mind/Body problem.

When one realizes that all is part of the divine then these hard distinctions become unnecessary. While they are not necessary these distinctions are useful for the egoistic consciousness to make discrete categories to describe the world which is useful in its telos to survive.

It's not important really to say that there is not a distinction between matter and energy any more than is it important to say there is no difference between dawn and dusk, winter and summer, heat and cold. These distinctions are the result of the manifestations of the eternal one, the infinite God.

Once again matter has its determinates as do biologically based organisms so a hard and fast distinction cannot be drawn between the thing that thinks and the thinking thing.

Yet it seems that we all must have freedom for if there were no freedom then God would be inert and life would be baseless.

The primordial God is bound by neither matter or energy, freedom or determinism. But since God is infinite this unity of Being must also be manifest in its myriad nature. But how do we get past the unmoved mover (e.g., God that moves itself)? Why does the mover move at all? Why would it move if its ultimate nature must be a non-discrete formless amorphous mass? What is the nature of existence? Can something exist that is unwitnessed? What would it mean to be something that exists only for itself but not for an other? Such a Being would have no identity. If God is infinite then God must have the potential to exist and this includes existing discretely in the cosmos. If something has the potential to exist and is infinite in its nature, then when looking at possible world semantics we know that in some way it must exist. Put another way, possible existence for the infinite makes existence certain. In the modal argument that if god is necessary and therefore possibly exists then God necessarily exists. In the same way if existence is possible if God is existence then existence is necessary.

This includes cosmic existence.

Does the cosmos seem to show the divine will? How does the cosmos seem to represent the action of divine Being in the world? When we look at the sky, we see stars, planets, distant galaxies and the appendages of black holes. All these things seem discrete and seem to exhibit some form of regularity at least to our consciousnesses. It seems like a firm case can be made that this manifestation of the cosmos can be all we can talk and all that is worth talking about which is said by the logical positivists. How can the idea of an infinite God fit within this assumed stricture?

One way to understand the logical positivists position and a logical way of looking at it in fact, is that they are the ultimate skeptics like the Buddhists who make no claim about the nature of God but don't feel it is useful to talk about such nature because there is no empirical evidence.

While this is a well-founded belief it leaves one with an endless conundrum because when talking about the nature of infinity one cannot explain its nature nor even begin to do so and therefore one lives for all practical purposes in a perpetual state of ignorance. It seems clear then that a more logical approach is called for.

While the criticism of the medieval scholastics seems well founded as demonstrated by Kant, taking the skeptical position can never allow one to assume a metaphysical foundation and therefore the epistemology of such a system seems fatally flawed.

While western epistemology is useful for the survival of the specie, ultimately this attitude of the preeminence of the human cogito results in widespread destruction of habitat and the general soiling of the human realm of experience.

So suffice it to say that not only is using the intellect to understand the cosmos and the nature of God important but rather it is essential. One might argue that it is only natural that this position is taken that there lays my natural inclination. My response is simply to look at the worldly degradation and decide for yourself. This is a foundational issue and cannot be simply traced to ethical concerns. This approach plagues the scientistic West.

So since God is ultimately the infinite then it must be of its essential nature for it to manifest itself especially to others. One problem of existence is that for something to exist there must be an other as the great master Hegel so clearly showed. One forms that opinion of themselves on how they see others. In a more abstract sense God can have qualities by manifesting them. Therefore for God to have a nature at all (in the cosmos) then God most exist spatially and temporally. Only in the spatial-temporal realm can things manifest themselves and therefore arrive at the "other".

So it seems natural, even essential, for God to have qualities there must be an other, and also in doing so these must be something that cognizes God.

While everything that exists is God, the order of things is such that Being can come to know itself. This is the goal or telos of physical as well as spiritual evolution. This is what I call returning to the source. And of course it seems reasonable at least for something to have identity that it must be perceived by an other. For if this other was simply understood by Being as itself understands itself then no identity would take place.

So certainly the egoistic consciousness must be blind in this process of knowing itself. While things are not really distinct between God and non-God, it must seem so at least from a cosmic perspective. Only then can the infinite manifest itself. It's really no matter that the infinite God or Brahman can not be differentiated primordially. This too is because of God's infinite nature.

60

So this ignorant thing is really as limited as it can be, as it is the finite apprehending the infinite. Such is the nature of opposites, birth and death, master and slave. But this is the only way that Being can come to know itself. This is necessary for infinite to manifest itself naturally. But in this process of being coming to know Being, God consciousness occurs. This then is the dream of Vishnu.

This then explains the identity of God.

The Teachings of Sri Aurobindo Reflect an Ideology of Up-rightness

The Yoga Party holds that the teachings of Sri Aurobindo reflect an ideology of up-rightness.

Since as stated before the ideology of the Yoga Party is not transcendental then it is not earth denying and other worldly affirming and therefore is not inverted but instead purports an up-rightness. Also similarly the ideology of the Yoga Party is not life denying nor death affirming. These are shown by the fact that just as spirit exists in our understanding of the beyond so does it exist in our understanding of the world.

In other words the teachings of Aurobindo reflect a human consciousness that recognizes this consciousness as an understanding of the ultimate Being being the same as one that is fully God-conscious. In a sense the only difference is by degree.

While the human ego dwells on the needs of its insentient matter for the bodies organization and survival one's limited human egos appreciation of outward and inward Being seems limited. This comes about because both the inward physical body and the external physical world both are in essence spiritual. That is both are a manifestation of the God-head which humans even in their most parochial outlooks contain a degree however blinded of God- consciousness.

Just as there is no sharp distinction between the physical inner self and the outer physical world also there is no difference between the inner self-consciousness and the outer-consciousness of the divine. Neither is greater than the other because each is part and parcel of the same primordial stuff. The only difference between the self and the world and the supernatural is a degree of understanding known through consciousness an understanding obscured by Maya.

62

Maya is very easy but also very difficult to understand. Once you grasp at it it is lost and if its mysteriousness obscures one's thinking than a cure cannot be found. Maya is ignorance. Once understood it dissolves. In the dissolution of Maya one comes to understand the limitations of the ego and becomes able to truly become God-conscious. There is no hard and fast dividing line between the immanent world and the transcendent world no sharp distinction between the mundane and the divine. In fact all is divine.

As the supposed distinction between the mind and body is illusion so is the supposed distinction between the mundane and the otherworld illusion. Descartes has shown that, although inadvertently that a fine line cannot be drawn between mind and body, so that while it may be useful epistemologically it is unsound metaphysically. It cannot be understood that an atemporal aspatial mind can interact with a temporal spatial body and therefore this distinction must be thrown out as shown by Occam's razor.

The question can be asked as to why it matters, whether it is important whether one's worldview engages other-worldliness or this-worldliness? Aside from the seeming fact that the other-worldliness is an untenable view, taking a this-worldly view which Aurobindo seemed to endorse implies a validation of the human condition in the world at this time which dwells in the divinity of all. This seems to be the only conclusion that can be arrived at at least one that makes sense.

When taking the position of this-worldliness, one affirms the earth while at the same time affirms God. In doing so one affirms human strength and the integrity of the egoistic will. While this may go beyond the methods of Sri Aurobindo let me say that the egoistic being being part of the physical and spiritual evolution, must adopt a position of strength through the egoistic will and only then can it achieve integrity as a being in seeming competition (in the Darwinian sense) with other organisms in the web of life. As

63

we emphasize spiritual evolution in Aurobindo's system, one cannot deny the physical evolution as well.

But through this transformation of Being one can realize the deterministic nature of the one; call it God both within and without. Without the illusion of Maya spiritual progress could not be made just as one could not achieve good in a world beyond good and evil, so the human condition dictates a sort of world in competition. But this does not truly separate the world from the divine.

The beliefs of Aurobindo do not imply that that which is transcendental is only that which is real. In order to take such a position one must deny the integrity of the world. This position has often been ascribed to the Christian religion, erroneously I think meaning that the Christian religion denies the world and only affirms the world to come. Many Christians claim that the world is only a proving ground for our coming transcendence, and this is why the claim is often made that Christianity is a religion of inversion rather than up-rightness, I think a position could also easily be taken that since the world is the creation of God, that the world shares in the divinity of God as Christ shares in the divinity of God. In this case the Christian faith could be understood as being in a state of upright-ness.

This position is not really a problem for the trials and tribulations of the world. As all struggle through the toils and troubles of the physically inspired egoistic consciousness when one realizes one's true nature then one comes to value ones physical evolution as being no different from one's spiritual evolution and even more importantly one comes to realize that essentially the two really are not different at all. That is because the world is every bit as real and Godly as the seeming world beyond. This then leads to evolution and the apprehension of the unity of all through God-consciousness.

This is why I say the teachings of SriAurobindo reflect an ideology of up-rightness.

<u>The Prison of Matter</u>

What do I mean by the "prison of matter"?

According to standard western metaphysical theory there are two discrete entities in the universe. There is matter and there is energy. Einstein made this much simpler when he posited a relation between energy and matter as E=mc2. In other words energy and matter are intimately related. Evidence for this is the atomic bomb where a small amount of matter is released as energy resulting in the well known mushroom cloud. Since energy and matter are so intimately related it would seem that the distinction between mind and body could be less dissimilar than is usually thought.

Nowadays science talks about mind as being little more than the firings of neurons. The chemical structure of the neural synapses either stimulates or inhibits inter-synaptic firing and these different firing patterns determines the overall brain activity. This seems simple enough. Mind then is simply a product of the firing of neurons. But can this be all there is to it?

Where does the concept of mind or its closely related supposition geist or spirit come from? From Descartes we have the mind and body. The mind acts freely by thinking, and we know the body must exist because the mind thinks thus the cogito "I think therefore I am." The mind historically has served as the ghost within the machine. The mind is indispensable for humans to be truly intelligent. Why? This is because to be truly intelligent and therefore thinking you must be free. How would a thing think if it was determined as all matter seems to be so by the determinants of physics?

Descartes Mind/Body solution seems to serve us well. It provides a way to use the mind to verify that what we perceive is in fact accurate. We use the nature of mind as a free thinking thing to show that the world must be as it seems to be even though we are often fooled as we are by mirages in the desert and the like. Included in this argument is the use of the rationality of the mind to arrive at the conclusion that the senses are not in fact fooling us. Of course then the freedom of the mind to think freely is indispensable. This would seem to only reinforce the notion of God who gives us ability to think freely.

This formulation by Descartes refers to a field in philosophy called Epistemology or Theory of Knowledge. We can have knowledge because we can know beyond any doubt that the world is as it is perceived so are not subject to error. That is the triumph of Descartes method that formed the foundations for science which have served the world so well. But while the Cartesian method excels in usefulness it fails from a philosophical perspective. The mind is posited as an immaterial substance while the body is said to be a material substance. The mind is aspatial while the body is spatial. They are totally dissimilar and never the twain shall meet! This then is a metaphysical consideration (e.g., talking about the nature of reality). So in fact while Descartes method is very useful it is impossible. One might ask what difference does it make if it works. Such is the position of the pragmatist.

But the pragmatists talk little about the nature of reality. But in my opinion this is an important question. If we cannot base the mind and body as being completely dissimilar, then we must posit it as somehow being similar. This is common sense.

Some might claim then that the example listed at the beginning is so important, the part where I talk about neural firing to explain brain activity. While Descartes attempts to explain the world through the rational mind, modern science tries to explain the action of the mind as being strictly the result of material processes. While this does not seem to be a problem for Descartes when thinking about it being necessary and sufficient when one thinks about it in detail we find out that the mind is no different from the body. In fact the mind is the body.

The instant the synaptic pattern fires, simultaneously we have a thought, memory or sensation. But the idea seems to be a byproduct of the synaptic firing. Yet it seems too that one could say that although seeming more incredulous that the idea caused the firing. Once again though if this is the case we find ourselves at the same problem as with Descartes, how does the immaterial mind impact the material body? So it seems clear that this conclusion must be rejected in favor of thought being the result of physical processes. But there is another problem.

If the mind is simply the result of the pattern of synaptic firing and therefore all material, then where does our freedom come from if all mind and matter are governed by physical processes? If we say that we "learn" from our childhood from exposure to the environment then it seems we can say that we can tap into this repository of experience for making choices about what is right and wrong.

I remember reading about someone who viewed a lamp. This lamp caused a certain pattern of synaptic firing in their brain. This activity was recorded. Then later they were asked to think of this lamp and it was found that the pattern of firing was similar although less pronounced of the original firing pattern. This then could be called an example of memory.

So we remember things as experiences first through the senses and later drawing on our store of these vast experiences to make intelligent decisions. This is not much different from a pack of wild dogs in which the young learn to hunt. But if our thought is just the result of our experiences then how can we have free thought? Everyone's experiences are different so under this theory everyone necessarily would act differently because their experiences are different. Where does free will come in?

68

Perhaps then it is a combination of the two what science calls nature and nurture. Nature would refer to our heritable endowment and nurture to our environment. This then some might say how we can have free thought we just adopt the best of both worlds. But it is clear that heritable characteristics would be deterministic as would experiential considerations. You hear of diseases such as schizophrenia which is thought to have a genetic component that lies dormant unless it is activated by a specific type of environmental factor. This boggles my mind.

How can the deterministic characteristics of DNA be activated by purely environmental factors? It seems if one wants to be picky we can understand that if DNA potentiality is activated by a specific type or types of environmental factors that this too must be a form of determinism. I mean after all the DNA, being physical, cannot "choose" what to respond to. The characteristic of stress resulting from the loss of a loved one, economic loss, or the result of the impact of war or natural disaster all result from a material basis of being of which all things are based on physical properties. Remember we were talking about firing synapses. There is no place for mind here. It would just be matter acting on matter after all wouldn't it?

I'm sure many are skeptical of the materialistic vs. idealistic quandary. We must have a spirit. Those that have lived through a great loss or pain are a human being damn it, they are the experiences of their life and their life is something authentic with meaning.

What would we have if our life was not in fact authentic? We could not have knowledge because knowledge implies free will. We could not "learn" from our mistakes. None would then be morally culpable for their heinous acts. A murderer who had no free will could not be called guilty of a crime because they did not act freely. In order to be guilty of a crime you must be rational and therefore have free will. This is why one cannot be found guilty if they are judged to be insane.

You could just be here reading this essay because you are determined to do so. In fact from birth to death your life would be deterministic perhaps the result of your genetics and your environment. I'm sure this is hard for someone to think about but can you really prove you think freely? You can't. The only way you could know you had choice is if you did an act and then went back in time and did the act in a different manner. It's all very depressing isn't it?

But there is another possibility. Rather than there being a sharp distinction between mind/body which Descartes posited or a material basis for all which seems to be the direction of modern science the other logical possibility (and seemingly the only one left) is that we and everything this is is all spirit or if you like better all mind.

You may not be convinced but remember the relationship posited by Einstein of the relationship between matter and energy, in essence matter is potential energy and if some theory's in cosmology are true, then energy is in turn potential matter (e.g., the false vacuum hypothesis). One might respond then that all is matter, but it seems more correct to say they are neither matter nor energy but something that is really primordial.

The only thing that is changeless is change. The more things change the more they stay the same. You may have heard these sayings before. Is change changeless, born of physical determinants?

We can't talk about infinity or finitudeness in the same breath. They don't seem to be at all connected. But things cannot be ultimately finite. This seems logical. For if things were finite how would they be bounded? We can think of a globe which we can traverse in any direction on an endless course around but this too seems limited because we tend to end up in some fashion where we started. If the universe expands infinitely then its density approaches negative infinity. Or we have repeated big bangs which seem to be determined by its "history?" Suffice it to say that we cannot draw a hard line between finity and infinity.

Does this mean that infinity does not exist? Infinity must exist, or it seems it must because if it did not then it would be finite. So perhaps it is our way of thinking about it our lack of understanding. Remember we are trying to get out of our bounded prison of matter. And get out we must if life is to be meaningful, and we are to be free beings.

While we cannot understand infinity we can understand the concept as something that is not finite. It seems clear that we cannot be simply determined matter otherwise the universe would be limited. But since the universe is unlimited it seems that we must in some manner be free. If we are just some inert mass of Being this too would be a limitation just as if Being were just pure action. So it seems clear that Being must be both action and inaction. It seems we have to throw out Aristotle's excluded middle, at least for this. But we can arrive at Aristotle's unmoved mover. The thing that moves itself. This would be the thing that is truly infinite, call it God or Being. But then again maybe not. We just threw out the excluded middle (can not be both so and not so). So God is either moving or it is not. It doesn't matter whether it moves itself, it is either in motion or not and not both.

As the revered Sri Aurobindo explains it, it is like a candle's flame. At the same time it gives off both light and heat. In this case the flame is the thing in itself and the heat is its effluence or action. It would be nonsense to try and separate the two.

It seems necessary to get past the knowledge constructs of the material world to escape determinism. Only then can we escape the prison of matter.

This is all I'm going to say for now about the prison of matter.

71

A New Voice

Since I seem to be a proponent of my own philosophical positions, I will claim to be beholden to no one except myself. I cannot be an interpreter of other positions, for example Sri Aurobindo so I must present his teachings in the way I understand them and not claim to be some sort of authority on his teachings.

Although I think his teaching are very useful, and I think they form an effective framework for world thought. I think it is presumptuous for me to try to speak something new for someone that has passed. Others as well including Aurobindo's followers may not appreciate me taking license with his positions.

So I will continue to use the framework as I understand it of Sri Aurobindo. As I understand it I feel I have a clear vision about how western philosophy can fit under his apt umbrella but still it would be presumptuous for me to talk as an authority about this great master.

So no longer will I refer the positions I expound as being Aurobindo's positions. It is merely hyperbole for me to claim that I can do so.

I think it is clear from my reading of Aurobindo that he alludes to the western philosophers, and he being classically trained in the West was well aware of these traditions perhaps more so than his knowledge of the traditions of his native country.

But of course there is East and West and never the twain shall meet. At least this is true in some eyes.

Also it is a fact that I really have run out of things to say from a strictly Aurobindo mode of interpretation. So since I don't want to take license with Aurobindo's works and I wish to expand my own, I have decided to take possession of all my works as my own original ideas which they may have been all along but unknown to me.

I need to speak for myself after all. I seem to have in fact found my voice. So I will hope to branch out in my presentation of the confluence of different philosophical positions without necessarily holding any as paramount.

But even now I find myself bound by the master. But suffice it to say that even Aurobindo in all his wisdom would not hold any belief as most important but only useful in understanding a larger truth. It's with this attitude that I will approach my work searching for the larger truth to which all belongs, finding the way things belong to all, and finding the truth in a sort of oneness or monism and multiplicity as well very different from the fragmentalized tradition that results from the nearsightedness of the individual pedagogical perspectives.

The Courting of Desire

Out of the end comes the beginning. From the beginning comes the end. Out of life comes death. Out of death comes the fertility of life. Yet life seems to endure beyond one that passes away. And change endures beyond one who in death becomes still.

When one comes to pay respect to the dead one is paying respect to life. They are celebrating that person's life and remembering how they were as they were when alive. Only the dead respect the dead.

Anger and suffering is the human condition. As the Buddha says "Life is suffering." Without a body how could one suffer? The ultimately irony is that life breeds suffering, a harbinger of death while death breeds peace. Why then would one prefer life?

Most often one lives as they die--lost. Anger and resentment, hate and brutality impinge on the senses. The desires of the senses teach us what is to be acquired and what is to be shunned. And when the desires are filled the thirst is never quenched. Beginning as a drop, to a stream, and into an impetuous flood pours the ocean of desire.

And when the killing starts it's for a slight, a misunderstanding, an insult a flippant joke. From the kernel of a seed grows the vines of hatred. "How dare they" one might mutter. "Damn them!" one might cry out loud.

And when the floodgates are broken and the outpouring of wrath streams outward war is born. Like earth and in heaven the great armies' only goal is to kill more efficiently, and the God almighty cries for revenge. Blood flows across the land and the rivers are dyed with turbid clay.

But then it ends. Enough have died. The senselessness of it all becomes apparent.

Or perhaps reduced to exhaustion the hate remains but one must nurture themselves to regain strength so the slaughter can begin once again.

And out of the putrid rotting flesh and burning blood the soils are replenished. Nature as it is able to revives itself as best it can. But as humans wreaked destruction on the earth, the earth may call back to them that they are no longer welcome. "Be off with you" it may say.

So the blood dries. But the biological toxins developed so as to be most effective in killing may kill again. And the chemical munitions used to burn the skin may infect the human genome affecting generations. Or the radiation will set into the soil and into ones lungs and genitals producing cancers and infesting the land till the end of the earth.

So as man creates, man destroys. The adaptive advantage of the human species has been the efficacy in which it kills. And babies are nourished to become soldiers in any future slaughter. This is the only function when the birth of the young exceeds those of generations before. Babies grow up to be fodder for the war machine killing babies that might one day challenge them. Sometimes disease can relieve this pressure as the bubonic plague did so efficiently. Now it is warfare and the allied weapons. But let's remember righteousness and holiness. These are the watchwords of those that pervert the rights of life. Only through wanton destruction can one know their fruits.

On Joy and Pleasure

There is a fundamental difference between joy and pleasure.

Pleasure is not to be avoided. Pleasure is part of the human condition. In fact pleasure ultimately is unavoidable.

Socrates in the Phaedo says that when his chains are removed in prison that he feels pleasure. In this case the pleasure seems to have come out of pain or discomfort. I think this firmly demonstrates that pain and pleasure are inexorably intertwined. We experience pleasure because of pain and pain because of pleasure. In fact the two are not fundamentally different in their essence.

Pleasure like pain is part of the mortal coil. If one looks at modern psychology when one has a painful existence especially psychological pain one seeks pleasure to remove the pain.

I always thought it interesting that the thing that is most pleasurable (even more so than an orgasm) is an intravenous injection of heroin (or so I am told). Yet the addict in their last stages of addiction experiences the greatest bondage imaginable and only injects the drug to keep the pain away. The pleasure has vanished.

This is not to say that pleasure leads to pain or pain leads to pleasure although both of these are possible but that once again that they are inexorably linked. Certainly a central position can and must be taken for ones serenity, and that is to avoid the extremes between the two in the act of acceptance.

What is the relationship then between pleasure and desire? Desire I think is wishing to possess pleasure. And pleasure reinforces in the sense of operant conditioning desire for the object that gives pleasure. Some think that this reduces to love. Certainly it seems clear that this is a form of what Kant refers to when talking about Pathological Love. Perhaps then because the object of desire is not novel,then the pleasure dissipates like the pleasure of the drug addict.

Such is the nature of pleasure

On the other hand joy is not extinguished through experience. Joy can be taken in the simplest thing and does not bind one. Joy includes the bliss of an enlightened consciousness. Joy is having companionship. Joy is being associated with someone that cares for you and you care for in return. This bond is not extinguished, and one that nurtures it and cherishes it will always have it and never lose it.

This then is joy and it is clear that joy is preferable to pleasure.

Spirit and Matter – Problems with Marx's Theory of Revolution

Marxism has become taboo in the West. It is not so much vilified anymore as simply being and aged an outmoded belief system. This is convenient for the capitalist who have a vital stake in getting people to accept this claim.

Marxism is considered subversive became it seems to promote the revolutionary overthrow of the status quo. According to Marx only through revolution can the crimes of the bourgeoisie be addressed.

Yet there seems to be a primary problem with Marxist theory. There are two primary views regarding the causes of revolution. There is the Class Struggle view and there is the view from the perspective of Historical Materialism.

Class struggle simply states that revolution is the result of the struggle between the classes, the bourgeoisie (the landed class) and the proletariat (the landless class). This involved free action of the proletariat against the excesses of the bourgeoisie in the struggle over capital (e.g., money). Revolutionary change involves free will.

The historical materialism view on the other hand says that revolution is the result of historical forces which are beyond the grasp of the capitalist classes (e.g., bourgeoisie and proletariat). In other words the nature of revolutionary change is deterministic.

So deciding the nature of revolutionary change, be it free or determined, is an important consideration. What then are the implications of this? If revolution is the result of free will then it becomes paramount for governments to suppress it if it is to maintain its hold on its surplus profit (the money it steals from the proletariat's labor). Active suppression is necessary. This includes arbitrary arrests, suppression of unions, restrictions on free speech, indoctrination of the proletariat masses with the capitalistic worldview.

The interesting thing about all this though is that Karl Marx was a materialist. According to Marx, ideas are simply the result of material forces. It is because of this that it seems that the class struggle view cannot be correct. In fact in essence thought is simply part of the materialistic process. This then perhaps is a weakness in the Marxian worldview. Why? Marx borrows his ideas from Hegel, in particular Hegel's masterpiece "The Phenomenology of Spirit." In the Phenomenology of Spirit the idea is that knowledge is the spirit or idea coming to know itself. This process occurs through logical transformations derived from Hegel's logic in which certain historical problems are surmounted.

Take for instance the "Master/Slave dialectic (e.g., logical transitions). In this Hegelian formulation, when two individual meet in a state of nature and behold each other one becomes the master and one becomes the slave. The master is one that values liberty over life and the slave is one that values life over liberty. So naturally from these positions the master asserts authority. This is the first logical movement.

Second the slave works for the master and the master lives off the slave rather like a parasite. Since the slave is the producer it is the slave only that comes to know the true way things exist in the world. On the other hand the master lives off the slave, appropriating the products of the slave and therefore learns nothing about the way of the world. So the slave gains wisdom while the master achieves nothing.

So at this point because of the wisdom the slave achieves the slave becomes able to throw off the master and because of the oppression the slave experiences at the hands of the master the slave no longer fears death while in fact the master has been softened by his life of plenty and leisure. So the slave shakes off the master as a dog might shake off a flea. This is the second logical transition.

Finally because of this the slave assumes the role of master and the former master is enslaved according to Hegel. Or perhaps instead one lives in a classless society in which all are masters of their own existence and are fully actualized in this existence and with there associations with each other, which seems to be the Marxist final transition. This then is the third logical transitions and the dialectic is considered completed and then begins again according the Hegel or is completed according to Marx.

The important thing is that Hegel seems to have the upper hand. Since he is talking about spirit these logical transitions that all experience is not bound by materialistic forces unlike Marx. The knowledge gained by spirit is real and the knowledge gained is meaningful. Why is this? As enumerated before if change is the result of material forces including ideas as the result of the interplay of material forces (i.e., commodity fetishism – the desire to possess material goods – as being the result of the capitalistic production of these material goods), then ideas like matter or rather as matter are determined.

So since under Marx all is determined then nothing is meaningful. We have no say in the change that occurs. The struggle between the proletariat and the bourgeoisie is for naught. The struggle and subsequent revolution means nothing. This is because all is determined. For one to have a meaningful life one must be free.

One might say then, of course we must be free! One cannot know though if in fact they are free. The only way is to commit and act then get into a time machine and go back in time and commit a different and contrary act. Of course we cannot know this.

But we know that things cannot be determined in themselves. For things to be determined there must be a determiner otherwise we are involved in an infinite regress (e.g., causes that have no first cause) or circular reasoning. There must be an original cause in either case. At least according to our limited worldview this would seem to be so.

For something to act there must be something that acts. For a flame to give off light (the thing in itself or noumena), it must give off heat as well (the thing for another or phenomena). So it seems clear Marx's theory is flawed.

For the world to exist – for an impersonal unity (e.g., God) to be all there must be a spirit that comes to know itself. This is the problem with Marx's theory of Historical Determinism and why one cannot be free if ideas are driven by materialistic forces and in fact therefore are material.

This is not to say that a Hegelian theory of revolution cannot be posited. Lets just suffice it to say that Marx's theory seems flawed

This explains the problem of Marx's determinism vs. freedom and demonstrates the superiority of Hegel's position.

A Cursory Examination of Finitudeness and Infinitudeness

If one can surmount the mundane existence then one can lead the blissful life. The trials and tribulations that trouble the world are no matter to the enlightened one.

As Schopenhauer observed if one person perishes life goes on. What worth is the individual? All live and all die. But we are never separated from the stuff of life. In the organs in the sinews in our sweat lies the essence of all being. When one escapes the prison of the egoistic self one is truly free.

No fear disturbs the enlightened one. Death is but a change in life as change abounds in the universe. All is change. In a sense change is changeless. Change seems to be random but out of this randomness comes order. What a mystery within a mystery.

In the egoistic self we are bound by a finitudeness. Released from the egoistic self we come to recognize this finitude as such. Both finitudeness and infinitudeness must exist, as light to dark, or short to long, or maximum to minimum. How can they not both exist?

A finitude without infinitude is nothing. Infinitudeness without finitudeness likewise is nothing. Infinitudeness cannot be if it does not have finite parts. What sort of thing would an infinite emptiness or nothingness be?

So the human creation must exist in infinitudeness. But infinitudeness cannot be grasped. For once infinitudeness is grasped one realizes that all things lie there. There can be nothing greater. But Aurobindo does state that neither is preeminent. Limited consciousness or not it is still consciousness. As the Buddhists say we are all Buddha's, we just don't know it.

Infinitudeness cannot be grasped by human consciousness. Humans exist as human and therefore are finite. When a bird sings, when lightning strikes, and when thunder roars it roars for us. As Hemingway says "when the bells toll it tolls for thee."

Infinitudeness must have finitudeness. For without finitudeness it could not be infinitudeness. With infinitudeness comes infinite possibility. If change was not random then it would not be infinite in nature. Randomness is not bound by any mechanism and therefore is free. Randomness in nature shows the infinitudeness of the absolute. It is this randomness which gives birth to the infinite possibilities in life and the universe.

The infinite cannot be understood but only realized. The senses are bound by the determinants of random creation. As the infinite works on matter or spirit infinite variations are achieved and this results in finitudeness.

One way to know the infinite is to think of it abstractly. The mind is composed of a physical structure in electrical motion. This is the bond between matter and energy and contrariwise. This makes free thought possible. In this case energy depends directly on matter. Energy is released from matter without a cyclotron. And in this energy lies thought or mind.

In our minds we have a sense of abstraction; we have the concept of the finite and the infinite. How can this conception be an illusion?

While infinitudeness cannot be understood logically or practically one can cultivate awareness through the exercise of the mind with the result of a divine nature. After all infinitudeness must in a sense be the divine.

Thus is a cursory examination of finitudeness and infinitudeness.

Unity and Division in Racial Attitudes

There is much variety in the universe. In fact it seems like things in the universe could hardly be more varied. This is due to the random nature of change. Like the physical structures of the universe, there is a myriad variation in life on earth and probably throughout the universe.

When we think of the organic and the inorganic matter of the universe we usually think of two different chemical properties. Yet it seems in fact that all is matter, the difference being that the inorganic matter does not support life but the organic matter does. Is this really a difference in kind or is it simply in function?

The same sort of analogy can be drawn in the kingdom of life. The world seems to be the perfect place to enable diversity. The healthier the ecosystem the greater the variety of life. The randomness of change in nature promotes an endless amount of diversity.

And all life is contained in its own niche. Humans have proved rather remarkable in that they have been able to climb out of their narrow niche and have multiplied greatly and have therefore been able to reach into other specie's domains.

All life is dependent on other life. One mistake that humans often make is that they think they are not bound by nature or are not even part of nature. Oftentimes in our technocracy it is thought that for every natural problem there is a technological solution. Time may not be on our side. But this is a subject of a different issue.

Humans are very narrow in the scheme of life. Like all species as the word species is defined all are able to mate and have fertile offspring.

When one talks about race they are actually talking about types that were created in Western Europe to justify white European

84

dominance of the distant colonies. By creating these racist categories it was posited that whites were superior intellectually and especially morally. But in fact there was no essential difference between Europeans and peoples of other parts of the world.

This division then was arbitrary and without a basis. The division is based on ignorance especially the ignorance of the egoistic self. These divisions are used to prevent people especially in the United States to think of themselves as radically different rather than as being the same essentially. This division serves the interests of the capitalistic masters in order to pit people against each other to lower wages and increase profits.

When people are judged morally based on physical characteristics then those that judge are racist. If one is thought to be lazy or evil based on skin color for instance then they are said to be racist. If one can recognize that these distinctions are created and only benefit the ruling class then one can begin to see the humanity of all.

In the universe the variety of things seems unlimited. As stated before so it seems with life. And divisions are made as well within humanity. The important thing to recognize in making racial distinctions is that we are part and parcel of the great expanse of Being and Time and all divisions ultimately are arbitrary and are only made when it serves the need of the egoistic conscience

Be True to Oneself

One of the most important things, if not the most important, is to be morally upright. When I talk about moral uprightness I'm talking most importantly about the golden rule: do unto others as you would have them do unto you.

This idea is clear to most peoples of the world, but another attribute of moral uprightness is to be true to yourself. What meaning can a life have if you are not true to yourself?

When one is true to themselves then one is authentic. When one is not then one is inauthentic. Sometimes finding what is authentic and what is not authentic in oneself is a difficult task. One is exposed to a barrage of Madison Avenue images telling you what you must want. One cannot help but be influenced by this.

How then is one to find their authentic self? One simple way (or maybe not so simple) is to find when you are acting out in an egoistic way. I don't want to restrict this to a penitent attitude. Certainly in an ideal world all would want to be respected and treated with respect. I think such a thing is possible, at least in an ideal world. In this world none would have to subjugate another. Strength a virtue not a vice. Strength must be affirmed.

But strength would not be necessary to demonstrate ones prowess when all acted toward the same altruistic attitude. When one acts for all all act for themselves. That is one who is authentic.

Certainly different people have different abilities. But all are the product of the transformations and permutations of the divine, brilliant and not so, strong and weak, beautiful and ugly. All depend on each other for their existence. For what is brilliance if most are more brilliant still? And what is strength if others are stronger?

Yes one must affirm life. Life is the churning and burning of the primordial matter and compass. All must be strong because to be strong is to be alive. To be weak and frail is something close to death. Even those meek religious disciples exhibit great power.

Let's affirm the earth as well as affirm the heavens. But let's be true to ourselves. For if we are not true to ourselves then we are a lie in a bottle. Our true nature would be denied. We must act by affirming ourselves. For to act otherwise weakens and deforms us.

Be true to your being. Perhaps not to be honest for honesty becomes dishonest, nor beauty because beauty eventually becomes ugliness, but affirm yourself, affirm others, be as you would be to the divine which created you and is you. Only then can one be authentic.

To destroy your neighbor destroys oneself. For one that would act against ones neighbor betrays oneself. As you cut yourself off from your neighbor you cut yourself off from your true being.

When you reject the humanity of others and only affirm ones own you destroy your own humanity. This is because you must lie to yourself for what you did. You might say I am superior or I am more righteous or I am more deserving. But all are deserving not just you. And when you blind yourself and bind yourself to yourself you descend into the darkness of denial. In binding yourself to yourself you almost relinquish your divine nature. You cannot move yourself and in the same respect you cannot stop your movement. You have become an island unto yourself. This is the punishment of inauthenticity.

But once inauthentic not always inauthentic. We are driven inward ever inward. We are taught the best world is our own and none other. This attitude has made transit across continents and around the world like a transplanted plant that when it takes root replaces what was there originally.

The rapaciousness of a creature triumphs not because it is right or just or good but simply because it acts as it does. Only sorrow waits for those that acquiesce.

87

But the story is not over yet. The rapaciousness has never ended.

The frontiers have been conquered. The wealth has been stolen. Now this being stands face to face with each other at the ends of the earth. The position of life becomes the position of death. Never yielding, acting for men and god all must perish to win.

Be right with yourself. Be true to yourself. If this fails you in life it will not fail you in death for only death awaits those who tarry so.

The Inculcation of Desire and the Scourge of Addiction

The scourge of addiction.

When one thinks of addiction they often think of drug abuse. This includes pharmaceutical drugs, illicit drugs and alcohol. But addiction is not limited to these.

12 step recovery programs have sprung up all over the country and all over the world. The programs focus on drugs, alcohol, gambling, sex addiction, hard drug addiction, overeating, smoking and even love.

Then there are programs for the partners or relatives of these addictions. They too are caught up in the addictive process. But are these all the addictions that we have?

Addiction comes out of pleasure. With addiction, the reward is transitory and fleeting. Addiction is a very human curse but its effects can be minimized. This is done through avoiding the triggers that bring to the surface the addictions.

If one is caught up heavily in the addictive process then the only way to escape is to practice the contrary. Like great chasms in the mind pleasure drives desire in our very synapses. In order for these synapses to atrophy they must no longer be stimulated, and the must efficacious way to accomplish this is to avoid stimulating them at all. They then fall off like the diseased branch of a tree that no longer receives nourishment from the trunk.

In the West addiction is a big problem. Here in the US we pride ourselves in that we live in the land of the free. This freedom includes the freedom to become addicted. That is we are free to become addicted if we harm no one else. We are free to fall into extreme depravity and perish without anyone lifting a hand. Such is the nature of freedom.

It seems that all have equal access to addiction. Addiction knows no class distinctions. From kings to paupers all are bound by desire. Why is this?

Being a capitalistic society, we are bred with desire. The consumers are inculcated with the desire to purchase the commodities that the laborers produce. These products are mass produced. In order to ensure consumption, advertising is displayed which drives consumption which drives the economy. Without mass consumption the economy would collapse. But we get mixed messages about how we should behave.

We may be taught to be frugal. "A penny saved is a penny earned." But meanwhile we are exhorted to buy buy buy. This results in individuals accumulating great debt which allows the usurers to make a handsome profit. All this leads to a great burden on the consumer.

As the desire to consume is encouraged, the worker must work harder and harder to satisfy this desire. Ultimately because of this desire the worker is driven like a beast. But the problem does not simply lie with the worker. The capitalist in their mechanizations is bound up like a drug dealer is bound by addiction and feeds the habit by addicting others. So none is free of this wheel of desire.

In order to support this ever increasing desire for material goods and thereby increasing consumption the needed goods of others around the world must be appropriated. This results in great poverty in the countries that have their wealth stolen and causes much suffering. This can and does result in bitter wars.

As John Lennon says in his rarely heard song "Working Class Hero" one is doped with religion, sex and TV.

Religion is effective because one denies this world and affirms the kingdom to come. This perspective can result in great destruction and suffering because the world is no consequence and anything that will hasten ones reunion in heaven with god is desired. One works on the earth as a sort of proving ground for

90

heaven. If one is good and follows the dictates of their elders and performs the required rituals then one is guaranteed a place in heaven.

Religion helps drive the capitalist engine because ones virtue is measured by the material goods one accumulates. One economic standing serves as a testament to God's favor.

Sex is also a big addicter. Sex is a natural drive in humans that often leads to procreation. In order to insure there are adequate workers in future generations to do the work and soldiers to fight the wars the kindling of the fires of desire must be stoked. But this results in problems too as one can become infirm from unfulfilled sexual desire. The objects of desire become never-ending fantasies or the urges are acted out in having a never-ending supply of sexual partners.

This behavior quite naturally is encouraged by the media. In combination with religion, sex can become especially pernicious. One's desire, while stimulated, must be repressed without satisfaction. This can result in all sorts of perversions. This results from the puritan ethic. This sublimation may be manifested and satisfied by substituting Thanatos (the death instinct) for Eros (erotic desire).

TV is the main purveyor of sexual material. But it is much more than that. Sex sells. From the scantily clad female with the bottle of beer to the attractive woman riding around in a new car teaching the TV's audience that satisfaction is achieved through the acquisition of material goods. But TV is much more than that.

TV teaches one what is socially acceptable what attitudes one should have especially toward consumption and of course that is to consume. All the houses are veritable mansions all the families dealing with petty problems in their perfect households.

Then there are the commercials. Well people call them commercials. But what commercials are are simply morals to the story which the TV play dances around. In fact it is the drama or comedy that one watches which is really the commercial. A certain sort of behavior is expected, what idols to idealize, what sort of people one should want to associate. Almost all the time exhibiting people of the conservative persuasion who serve as role models for the viewer.

TV is really the primary medium that is the driver of advertising. Usually billboards and magazine ads serve as only adjunct material to the TV ads. In driving advertising TV is selling desire. This really is the main tool that drives the capitalistic machine. Freedom, a common theme of TV screen plays set the standard of what one should expect in society and effectively translates this into all the different standards of addiction which bind the consumer to the production that drives the economy.

The driving of desire in capitalist ideology cannot be entirely avoided but can be minimized. One possible strategy would be to turn off the TV.

This then is a few words on the inculcation of desire and the scourge of addiction in American society.

The Sacred and the Profane

There are two fundamental perspectives regarding governance. There is the religious and there is the secular. Both are dogmatic in approach. Fundamentalist religious groups view the secular as profane. The secularists view the fundamentalists as dogmatists, that is having unjustified beliefs rather than having true doctrine.

Religion is famous for making judgments in spite of Jesus' pronouncements that none should judge. This judgment of the fundamentalists that the secularists are profane is as much a error as the secularists judging the fundamentalists as dogmatic for both the fundamentalists and the secularists are dogmatic (e.g., having unfounded beliefs).

In order for one to function in society one must adhere to certain norms. These norms define our attitudes toward government and the world. This is true of both the fundamentalists and the secularists. So in this sense at least the two are not so different.

While the secularists do not necessarily eschew God they consider that to have God in the public square is an affront. The primary logic behind this is that when a society is not founded on religion, that it is not provides the impetus that prevents oppressive theocracy. When a society is founded on equality and justice, as the secularists claim, then the government treads lightly on its people and peace and prosperity results.

But religion is not necessarily oppressive. One only needs to look at the great Ottoman Empire, or even modern Iran, where different religions live together in peace. It is only when the religious beliefs becomes so hardened that it won't allow for any diversity; this is when freedom suffers. One example might be Saudi Arabia.

But freedom can suffer in a secular state too. God is not a necessary proscription for oppression any more than a secular state. Great misery can result too in a secular state as well when the beliefs become hardened and no diversity is allowed. An obvious example of a secular state that oppressed its people was Stalinist Russia. Yet up till recently at least the US has lived in a secular society with a decent modicum of freedom. This may be changing with the battle in the public square for dominance. Take for example the fight over religious symbols on public property.

It seems clear that both the secular and the fundamental can lead to extremes. And it is clear that both as I've stated before are susceptible to dogma. The fundamentalist embraces lofty principles such as love your neighbor as you love yourself. The secular in the US talks about freedom for all based on enlightenment ideals. These ideals are traced back to the teachings of the ancient Greeks.

The basic difference then is that the religious embraces the heart while the secular stimulates the mind. What is superior then the head or the heart? Is it better to love or understand? To decide on one or the other is a non-sequitur because of course both are essential; that is both are part of being human. All humans love and have compassion as well as understanding. In fact one comes to feel compassion when one for example understands the plight of someone less fortunate.

The flag or the cross, which is to be the symbol of a society? Oftentimes the flag is carried and planted on conquered land made by a great sacrifice by the soldiers in service to God. One can fight for God or the Flag but the two are not mutually exclusive. Nietzsche speaks of the fact that the embrace of freedom in western society is the result of the oppression of the now dominant religious groups when they were persecuted in their infancy. So in fact secularism and fundamentalism seems to compliment each other.

But when these two groups are divided by politicians for political expediency then all lose. If a ruler is proclaimed to have a divine right then secularism flies out the window. Then the state and the religion are inexorably bound. The government can pound the drums of threats to freedom and in doing so can sound an alarm with both the secular and the fundamental. But in this alliance with the heart the thinking being is lost.

In this heartfelt state the passions can be stoked and the fear of losing their prophets to the enemy emboldens them. Then only through service to God can one save themselves and perhaps find a place in the heavenly beyond. And in this excess the public square is appropriated by force and parochialism reins in this day. This can result in great purges and punishments because when passions are inflamed revenge cannot be far behind.

Was Jesus a fundamentalist or a secularist? It may be thought that clearly he leaned with the fundamental. But Jesus was more than just a teacher or even a son of God but was also a revolutionary preaching against the worldly persecution of the Jews and proclaiming a great beyond where all might escape and live with God. While Jesus was a man of great compassion he was also a great thinker. One only needs to look at the parables of Jesus to realize that not only was he "a" son of God but was also the most prominent philosopher of his time.

The sacrifice on the cross of Jesus only become central to the Christian belief system later as Jesus was represented as the Lamb of God where we all should wash ourselves in his blood. What became more important than his teachings was his martyrdom. This is where the wisdom has been supplanted by the heart.

While many Christians pay lip service to the teachings of Jesus, the primary consideration is to defend his honor and in doing so finding one a place in heaven. Jesus spoke of love, but he also spoke of hypocrisy and the suffering of the poor. Out of his heartfelt pronouncements came profound moral teachings.

These moral teaching seem to be lost in the modern world. Interested parties and governments instill in the people that they must defend their prophets as they defend their nations. In doing this there is formed an unholy alliance between religion and politics. Each thinks they get what they want. The fundamentalist a place in heaven and the politicians' new lands of conquest and plunder under the guise of the nations accepted religious symbols.

The heart has survived but the mind has died. The new kings rule absolutely but then the peasants must suffer and perish.

The Earthly Self and the True Self

The earthly self and the true self are very different. The earthly self is drawn into itself. It does not realize it higher nature. When the self is bound to the earth and views itself as individual then this is what we call the egoistic self.

The egoistic self is very important in capitalism for it is drawn on the concept of the individual self. The state in fact reinforces this concept although blindly. We do not easily see ourselves as part of a greater Being.

It is a natural state to see oneself as an individual. Our physical and biological evolution depends on this. Our worldview is determined by this natural state. If things were not in a state of change then we would not recognize the self as such.

The state reinforces this drive for individuality. For one thing we are taught that it is a good to possess individual commodities produced by the market. We are taught to need these commodities as individuals. Perhaps you've heard of one "keeping up with the Joneses." Because of our blindness to the true nature of material things we identify and accept material goods as separating us from each other. The primary material good we identify ourselves with is our physical body.

To take this simply according the Aristotle form determines function. The state of our physical anatomy is driven by the needs of the individual as an individual in the world. One can look at Darwin's evolutionary theory for example. If this were not so then we would be maladaptive and perish. So the individual is inexorably bound by the physical qualities of nature and thus for the individual egoistic self to survive it must establish psychic boundaries.

One problem with traditional Hinduism is that there is the emphasis on seeing the world in a sense as illusory. This denies our individual nature which in fact is not an illusion.

The main thing to realize is that we see things very narrowly. Our glimpse of the true nature of things is obscured. But if we enlarge our consciousness we can both function as an organism in our earthly domain and as well appreciate the things that become apparent with greater consciousness. We can appreciate a higher reality which we all belong. There is no need in fact the earthly self must not be torn asunder from the face of the earth. We can and must have then the best of both worlds, the mundane and the All.

The State of War

It's no doubt that hate sells. One always wants to see someone else's dirty laundry (i.e., scandals, great financial loss etc.). We seem to get some sort of satisfaction in this or at least many of us do. Why is this so?

One thing that happens is that we feel superior to the one that is suffering. We are glad it is not us and it seems to validate our existence. When the US is thinking of bombing another country someone might remark that we should bomb them back into the Stone Age. Or we might say that we should turn them into glass (e.g., a nuclear attack). Many or most people don't object to seeing the suffering of others. In capitalistic societies we find ourselves in competition with each other and we generalize this idea into all aspects of our lives.

The primary reason for ones delight in the suffering of others is that we see ourselves as individuals. When someone dies a horrible death we don't feel any sort of bond to the one that dies. This can come about because of nationalistic considerations, racial considerations, religious considerations or class considerations or any other sort of arbitrary construct.

In order to make this distinction we must posit our own group membership. In a sense we are "owned" by different groups. Groups can be useful in ordering our lives. Many people are employed and so are members of an organization that produces some goods for sale. Group membership is essential for our survival. Group membership enables us to received support from different group members and has other general prerogatives of the group. But when the group becomes the basis for selfish gain only then do others suffer.

In capitalistic societies one finds each other in direct competition for survival. This is what is called Social Darwinism because supposedly only the strong survive. One only has to look at Darwin's theory in that strength is not really a factor at all but only being adaptive. If the salinity of the sea increases for example then maybe a certain algae will die and this is in no way dependent on the algae's strength but only its ability to adapt to its surroundings. Oftentimes though the "strong" succumb. One only needs to look to the extinction of the dinosaurs.

But one must belong to groups to survive at least in modern societies. And one must only be dependent on ones own actions as individuals in order to provide for our children. This is common more so in the atomic family than the extended family. Nevertheless even in a highly regimented capitalistic society one must still be able to recognize that they belong to the human race and must accept their humanity. Then one can shake off the satisfaction that one feels when seeing others suffer.

When we realize that we are driven by the same cosmic forces have the same dreams and want a peaceful and happy life can one understand that we must recognize the humanity of all or the human race as a whole may find itself in peril. Without this recognition we always live in a state of war and impending destruction.

The American Caste System

The United States economic stratum is said to be made up of classes. This is different or so it is supposed from the Indian economic system which is a caste system, although the Indian caste system has been liberalized through the efforts of Mahatma Gandhi.

While the Indian caste system seems to be becoming more liberal the US class system seems to be becoming less so. In fact the US system seems to be becoming a new sort of caste system.

The difference between a class system and a caste system is that in a class system one has upward mobility while in a caste system one does not. It is questionable if there still exists any reason to say that upward mobility exists in the United States except in very extraordinary cases.

Certainly we live out the American Dream. If one is hard working one can become rich and successful. Is this still true? While some might succeed, take for example Bill Gates but one forgets that he was the progeny of well educated parents. It is well known how he started his company working out of his garage and then became the richest man in the world.

Even assuming one is light complected is upward mobility assured for the hard worker? It is often said that one only needs to pull themselves up by their bootstraps, but it appears if one does not have access to a decent education then one is consigned to the trash dump.

One reason I say that the US is more of a caste system that a class system is that the poor are demonized for their lot. If someone is poor then "they made bad decisions" and "we regret the decisions they made" without considering our own economic prerogatives. They might even be characterized as having a moral failing such as being shiftless, lazy, a drunkard, or and idiot and therefore one that is not favored by God. This is similar to the way it was looked at in the Indian caste system where ones humble caste would be the result of some excess in past lives.

It seems today that the rich are young forever and beautiful, while the poor are old decrepit and ugly. The rich can commit all sorts of crimes known as white collar crimes but the poor commit street crimes like drug addiction and distribution and be sent away to live for years in solitary confinement in supreme prisons. The rich on the other hand go away to less prestigious country clubs than they have in their gated communities.

It's funny when I talk to people and they tell me that racism is on the wane. It is my belief that racism is a way of perpetuating classism. People don't see the faces of the poor; the poor blacks, Latinos and whites because they live in different neighborhoods. If there are poor whites then the rich can say that they have addressed racism. While the percentage of each minority group is greater than the lighter complected in poverty, the whites make up the majority of the abject poor. The rich then can claim that while we may not have completely addressed racism you can see there are an ample number of poor whites and this provides some evidence for a sort of reverse affirmative action reflecting favorably on the minority lower classes.

With the dissolution of the middle class, upward mobility becomes very difficult and probably impossible. I expect if the skills of the poor become too remedial then they can be flushed down the toilet and through the sewers into the polluted seas.

There is no compassion for the poor. Supposedly having compassion is coddling them. If you don't let them stand on their own two feet they will fall. I heard it said once that the rich would take a crutch away from a cripple and then claim, "look his leg has straightened out!" Such is the plight of the poor.

Karl Marx made the observation that the poor work and don't get paid and the rich don't work and amass all the wealth. The rich claim that the poor need to be taught to work, that a hard life will build character. It is easy to see the irony in this position.

Unfortunately a skyscraper without a foundation must collapse. All the minions can be threatened and cajoled but if they cannot endure the work and become unwilling to work, that they suffer so much that when their life is threatened they care not for the consequences, and then the rich will feel the poor's wrath. May the rich learn the lesson of other corrupt regimes and instead of repeating history reaping the hollow harvest of their actions.

Revolution and the Christian Death Cult

Revolution is not necessary. At least in the ordinary way revolution is thought of. Violence is never an option. Even if violence pointed toward victory it would be setting a bad precedent. A movement established by violence is based on a violent tradition. A history of violence results in a future of violence.

The USA for instance is a very violent culture. This is no surprise since it is founded on slavery and genocide. One might think that such a culture is superior because it has spread and supplanted much. The main reason though why this violent tradition has spread is because it is more effective in destroying its opponents and its opponents have been eliminated. This is not a judgment of the tradition, just simply a statement of fact.

Evolution determines the path of humankind. Each change in human history is determined by its past as well as present circumstances. The dominance of certain cultures has resulted in the elimination of peaceful ones nowadays most cultures are those cultures that have a history of violence. The peaceful cultures that have been lost would find a fertile soil today but they are long gone.

One cannot allow for further world wars because of the dire consequences. The world is armed to the teeth. There is a passé tradition called MAD which was in vogue during the cold war between the former Soviet Union and the USA. MAD stands for Mutually Assured Destruction. It was thought that it was somehow an advantage for two nations in this case two that were equipped with thermonuclear weapons in that they would not attack each other because mutual destruction would result. This was a deterrent to any sort of attack. This shows the insanity of modern weapons policy.

It is thought today by the ruling elite in the US that none can attack us and harm us because our position militarily is so superior to other nations. But in the meantime nuclear technology is readily available to other nations and the US can be attacked if such weapons can be smuggled in to the US. Also a terrorist attack on a nuclear power station would result in terrible destruction.

Nevertheless the US has threatened to use tactical nuclear weapons against Iran. The use of nuclear conventional weapons is accepted by many in the US establishment. This is a radical change in strategy which is certain to result in changing attitudes toward the use of such weapons around the world. This is very similar to the change in the US posture regarding first strike policy which has advertently resulted in the recent crises with Iran and North Korea. The US long thought a moral leader now sets the standard for immoral aggression.

In addition to this aggressive posture coveting world control comes naturally the lack of regard for quality of life. Capitalistic fervor manifests in the desire for world control is resulting in a steady decrease in the valuing of life and degrades living condition for all including those of the ruling elite. Now with the rise of the evangelical right and its emphasis on increasing population and the destruction of other species and environmental degradation this has caused a continuing degradation in the quality of life. While some people might be inclined out of self interest to turn back and address the needs for survival of the human species with the growing influence of the evangelical right the emphasis is on material possessions as showing God's favor results in an ever increasing extent of environmental destruction. In order to rationalize what is obviously impacting the world's environment some evangelicals have gone so far as to put faith in the coming rapture which will lift the believers off this putrid planet. There is even an impulse among the evangelicals to hasten this destruction so as to allow the rapture to begin.

105

Such a movement cannot be met with force. This movement has no compunction against taking the lives of the infidels. In fact to take the lives of the infidels may in their view be taken as a show of their devotion to God.

The world is dominated by the destroyers. Largely those that emphasize peace have long been destroyed. Those that compose the destroyers have developed more effective weapons as they delight in killing. How can we develop weapons more effective when the weapons that already exist threaten all life on earth? Rather it seems more effective in fact it seems to be the only option to develop ones consciousness and erase from our being hatred and fear. Perhaps the haters will destroy you but in doing this they may become aware that by destroying you they are destroying any hope for themselves.

In understanding the limitation of the worldview of the egoistic self one can see that holding on to life desperately is simply a way of denying the all of All. While taking a peaceful perspective may make one another target of the destructive perhaps some can be made to see the futility of their own position. It is clear that destruction which has enabled the spread of the violent around the world is not an option now as the violent face each other at the precipice. Those that fear for the self may in fact be persuaded, although the emphasis in a Christian death cult is becoming more and more prominent. Perhaps we can try and remind them that the religion is based on love and charity and perhaps the final calamity can be avoided. Hopefully then a violent revolution can be avoided and instead a spiritual revolution may take place.

Hindu Being and Buddhist Void as Metaphor

In Hinduism there is the One. In Buddhism there is the Void.

This seems to make Hinduism and Buddhism very different. While Hinduism considers Buddhism an offshoot of Hinduism, Buddhism considers itself to be quite unique. How can we reconcile these two?

Both Hinduism and Buddhism accept the doctrine of reincarnation. It's very easy to see that there is something to be reincarnated according to Hinduism. In Buddhism on the other hand the stuff of reincarnation in Buddhism seems to be absent because of the doctrine of the ultimate reality as being the Void. This is a problem for Buddhism and not Hinduism. In fact how in a godless universe can you explain existence at all coming out ex nihilo? Could Buddhism be a modified form of creationism? I'm certain the Buddhists would not agree with this but nevertheless.

It seems that each time a person is born that one's karma draws the personality inside. Karma exists but has no substance. Yet things seem to exist when in fact they do not. This must be true because the ultimate reality is the Void. Nothing is essential and without anything that is essential when the karma is gone this unstable being collapses into nothingness while still living one's life.

It is thought by some that the Void in fact is simply a sort of metaphor and that it does not in fact imply a sort of nihilism. Yet the example given by the Buddha himself is that Nirvana is like blowing out the flame of a candle. The question is where does the flame go? The answer is the flame is extinguished. This is a metaphor for life itself. When life ends oneself is extinguished. Is this talking about the end of life as surrender into the Void, or is this very similar to the view of the logical positivist in the West when life is over consciousness ends?

There is no creator God in Buddhism, at least not in the Teachings of the Elders (Theravada Buddhism). But here again perhaps this denial of God is simply a metaphor as well, when denying God the purpose is to reject something that is not important and is not actually a statement about metaphysical construct of the universe and ultimate Being at all. One only needs to think of the parable of the arrow where one has a poisoned arrow impaled in their side, it is fruitless to talk about the arrow, but rather the most important thing is to pull the arrow out, the arrow symbolizing metaphysics, and the removal of the arrow as a demonstration of the importance to deal with suffering in the world without analyzing the nature of Being.

So what is the Void? An obscure God? A metaphor? Or is it a metaphysical reality? One might be inclined to take the position that it is simply a rejection of the excesses of the Hindu priests rather like Martin Luther rejected the indulgences of the Catholic Church. This rejection of Being as all would naturally then be adopted as the Void in reaction. But once again is this a metaphor? It seems possible to think of it as a difference in terms but not a difference in Being. After all pure Being cannot be anymore talked about than the Void. The concepts are at root mystical. Hegel makes it very clear that to talk about pure Being and pure Nothingness as the same thing. Nothing determinate comes out of each individual concept. So perhaps adopting the Void as a metaphor may seem to escape this quandary.

But there is definitely taking a stance as a way to look at the world and perhaps this is the most significant difference. Buddhists, not bound to anything (i.e., pure Being) can be in the moment. Also they are responsible in the world and they can make a choice whether to be a Buddha in action (we are all Buddha's but we just don't know it) or we can still live a life bound by suffering.

So here again this seems to be taking a metaphysical position regarding the Void. But this really seems to be a metaphorical position as well for the Void is indeterminate. Without a determination or attribute it is really meaningless to talk about and can only be known through true experience. This is the same with Hinduism and Brahman.

Whether one is bound to Being in Hinduism is another question. Once again it seems that to take the position that Hindu's are bound to Being is more metaphorical than metaphysical because Being binds nothing to itself and cannot because nothing is not it. In order to be bound there must be a binder and something bound. Nevertheless Buddhism is very important and unique. It is a rejection of the excesses of Hinduism and the caste system and puts responsibility on all people in the here and now. The mistake made in traditional Hinduism is that one's position as Priest enables one to provide solace to the masses but this is a manifestation of the egoistic self and has nothing to do with the nature of Being. This position enables one to assume a sense of superiority that is unfounded and this is impossible metaphorically in the Buddhist tradition.

Have we decided whether the Buddhist Void is a metaphysical construct or a metaphor? Buddhism never rejects metaphysics outright, but calls it unimportant. This then demonstrates that the position Buddhists take in the world promoting independence and egalitarianism shows that the concept of the Void in Buddhism is important simply as a metaphor without taking a defined metaphysical position, and that this is quite simply a reaction to the excesses of the Hindu priests and does not differ in kind from Hinduism metaphysically.

Spirit, Matter and the All

In traditional Hinduism when one talks about the spirit one is referring to the All. The All is that which encompasses all things. Nothing can be removed or added to the All. So when one talks about the spirit one is not talking about a soul in the Christian sense. In traditional Hinduism that which is real is the All but that which constitutes the world is illusion. In the Christian sense when we talk about the spirit we are talking about that which "inspirits" us and gives us life and even more importantly human rationality. It is through this light of God that we are able to think. In traditional Hinduism on the other hand that which is the rational part of our nature is very confined and bound by ignorance, only through consciousness can we really understand the nature of Being.

Matter is not a part of spirit according to traditional Hinduism. Matter is ultimately part of the ignorance that results from our separation from God according to traditional Hinduism. The problem that results though is how can Being be all and yet the illusion of matter be not? Even something that is an illusion must be distinct from the All and therefore the All or Being is not All. This dichotomy is a great source of confusion. The idea of traditional Hinduism has not found a way to understand matter or put another way this illusion of Being. This results in a bipolar and bifurcated relationship between Being and matter which also exists in the West.

In the West this bipolarity is manifested as a body that is ensouled which drives the physical form. In this case matter is not an illusion like traditional Hinduism but the problem of the relationship between spirit and matter still exists. While traditional Hinduism tries to explain this by positing that the material is illusion, in the West the spirit or soul is what drives us and is the life constituent in each human being. In the West souls are individual like the bodies themselves.

While traditional Hinduism tries to solve the problem of spirit/matter as matter being ultimately illusion in the West the mind/body aka the spirit/body relationship is taken for granted. Whether one in the West believes that each person has a soul nevertheless most people in the West feel that there is a life force that drives the physical body. Evidence for this is the belief in the West that when the body dies consciousness ends and therefore the life force is lost. The belief is that there is nothing in physical matter itself that drives the body.

Nevertheless it is clear that when life leaves the body the body rots. So if this life is not spirit then what? Yet nothing lives forever. As things are born things die. From ashes to ashes dust to dust. Everything that is born is meant to die. And everything that dies nurtures the seed. One body's excrement is another flowers nurturance. The carnivores feed on the other animals. Other animals feed on the plants, the plants thrive from the fertility of the soil and death replenishes the plot. What then can we say about life and the spirit?

Even in inert matter the electrons fly around the nucleus of the atoms and the structure of the molecules are being transformed.

The universe explodes and being begins. The burning of hydrogen in the suns becomes heavier metals and when stars run out of fuel they explode spreading differentiated matter throughout the galaxies. Our physical atomic structure is the result of the decay of stars. The matter of life began there.

In traditional Hinduism, calling matter illusion denies the reality of the world. What would spirit be without matter? How can there be a differentiation of spirit without a differentiation of matter? Without matter pure Being becomes an inert "lifeless" stuff. Matter is no more being bound to the flesh any more than Being is bound to nothingness. Being and matter depend on each other and in fact are both essential to manifest.

It is clear in the West that in the ecological cycle no distinction is made between matter and life. All depends on all. In cosmology life seems like an accident. But when one considers the variability of the atomic structure of carbon based life one only need look back at the origin of the universe the big bang as the origin of life. Not only that but it is conceivable that other types of life may exist that don't depend on the carbon based model at all.

There then is no need to make a distinction between the spirit, matter and the All.

Religion, the Spirit and Evil

What is Religion?

Religion is different things to different people.

Religion usually refers to a specific set of dogma which forms the foundation for belief.

But is religion exclusive?

It is thought in the West often that one's religion is the only truth. All others fall into error. Therefore some religions feel they embrace the true God and that those that think otherwise are ill informed or even worship a false God. Even the claim is made that those who believe in a false God worship evil or Satan himself.

Religion is often grounds for war. In the West it is to protect the memory of the martyr most often Jesus Christ.

Emphasizing the spirit rather than an anthropomorphized type of God involves little if any dogma which one must adhere to. Spiritualism excludes nothing. My former lead faculty informed me once that he doesn't have one of those. But what is spirit? Is it dogma? It depends on how you define spirit. In the evangelical movement in the West the spirit means the holy spirit of God as they understand God. I think it is safe to take a more catholic way of looking at spirit.

In the West we often think of spirit emanating from God and as holy. But the western view takes an anthropomorphic view of God. I don't think that talking about spirit as God and holy is a problem. But according to my understanding of Sri Aurobindo all is spirit and therefore all is God and is therefore holy.

God does not really have a personality nor does God judge. The result of existence is a manifestation of the creative aspect of God. But God is more than that because God is all. God at the same time creates and is the creator and destroys and is the destroyer. We can think of God as all there is or as being pantheistic or as being individual and therefore ethical. But in not anthropomorphizing God one does not anthropomorphize evil as the devil either. God is no more human than God is a world or an eternity or a flower. God is all things. And to talk about spirit which my lead faculty did not seem to understand does not posit a sort of ghostly presence that lurks among us. Spirit is simply another name for God which all things are.

We cannot be evil in the western sense because we are God. God can do no evil that is we are divine.

So then what is evil? Evil is being blinded about our God nature. God does not persecute us or judge us or send us to hell. If God did this then God would in fact be doing it to herself because all is she. When we talk about evil as us being blind to our God nature this does not involve being immoral it is just our separation from God. We are God already and if we don't realize our own God nature then we suffer and cannot be happy. We lack knowledge about ourselves which we need to be fully conscious. This then is the sin, not realizing ones true nature and therefore not experiencing the bliss of one's own God consciousness.

The Antinomy of the Ultimate and the Other

How can we understand Being as One and Becoming as Another? When talking about God in the Hindu sense one says God is all. But when talking about all that is, one is not talking about what can be created. This seems to point to some confusion. If everything that is is the One or God or Being then how can this produce something different from itself? If it only produces itself then if that which it produces is itself then has it produced anything at all? For something to be produced that which is produced must be something different from that which is the producer.

Another similar problem is that which is oneself and that which is another. If one is oneself but oneself is part of the One or God or Being, and the One or God or Being is all then how can one say they are themselves at all? Traditional Hinduism sides with the idea that our perceived differences are only the result of illusion or ignorance, and if we were aware of our true self then we would see we are the same as all that is. That is we would see that all is the One or God or Being. Yet if the self is illusion then how can the One be real? For to understand an "all" there must be a multiplicity of things or so it seems. Or if the idea of self is illusion where does the oneness of all begin? It seems without a beginning there cannot be a One at all. We can of course attribute this to the mystical nature of the One, or God or Being. The skeptics claim though that if something cannot be talked about in words then you are probably not talking about anything at all.

Similarly in these two examples how can the One or God or Being be a thing for itself and at the same time for another (e.g., the cosmos, the world, the egoistic self)? In the first example from this section we have a thing in itself that produces another. But the question was if something in itself is All or God or Being, then how can it produce something different from itself? In the second example if the only thing that is real is the One or God or Being, then how can there seem to be a universe or cosmos that seems to exist? It seems under the traditional Hindu formulation that that which seems to be real is not (e.g., the cosmos, the world or the self), and that which seems not to be real is (e.g., the One or God or Being). This certainly seems counterintuitive.

Buddhism tries to simplify this problem by saying the flame of a candle is a metaphor for life. When a new life is reincarnated it is like taking one lit candle and using the flame to light another unlit candle thus lighting it then blowing the flame of the first candle out. This then is a never ending process. Yet Buddhism as well talks about death using the candle analogy as well. When one no longer has karma one is not bound to the world and therefore is no longer reborn. The metaphor for this is that the flame of the candle is blown out. The flame goes nowhere and is extinguished.

In Buddhism then the only thing that exists that can continue existence is karma and the ultimate reality is the Void so there is no need to talk about the One or God or Being because they do not exist and the only thing that does exist is impermanence – a sort of oxymoron. We don't need to talk about the world as existing as well as the One or God or Being because they all are useless talk. The Buddha seems then to avoid the problem of the relationship between the thing in itself and the thing for another produced (e.g., there is no thing) or the relationship between the One or God or Being and the world (e.g., all are part of the void and its beingness [the cosmos or the world] is just illusion). Yet karma seems to exist and to drive this wheel of existence, so what can we say about this karma? Can karma be an illusion as well?

Hinduism does not have this problem with karma. Karma is part of the nature of things. One's rebirth is dependent on one's past birth and therefore has a relationship to the One or God or Being. Yet the problem still exists between what we can call that which is the One or God or Being and that which it produces. For karma to

116

be real it must be part of the One or God or Being. Yet to have karma, for example one has human form. We have already decided that to have human form and to embrace the egoistic consciousness one must deny the One or God or Being. How can the individual and the All be the same?

Sri Aurobindo deals with this antinomy when speaking of the One or God or Being that when one talks about creation there is the creator and the thing created, or when one talks about the One or God or Being and the multiplicity of the world or when one talks about karma and the void as in Buddhism or when one talks about karma and the One or God or Being one only needs to think of a candle and its flame and its effluence of heat and warmth.

One can think of the flame and its effect warmth as being like the One or God or Being and the thing produced. Or one can think of the flame and its warmth as being like the One or God or Being and then the manifestation of the cosmos and humans herself. Or one can think of karma and the Void likewise because when a candle in turn passes its flame to another it seems to exist but does not when blown out reunites with the ultimate (e.g., the Void) and when the karma of traditional Hinduism is extinguished to become the One or God or Being we can be clear that that which is reunited with the One or God or Being is real so long as the candles flame spreads light and warmth in the world.

Thus discussed is the antinomy of the Ultimate and the other.

The Logic of Being

Is the logic of philosophy sufficient to understand the nature of Being? One question that seems to come first is is logic part of nature or is it a human construct? Logic in the past was the domain of the philosopher. Certainly mathematics is logical. Einstein felt that his theories adequately mapped reality. Unfortunately, like the previous cosmologists, Einstein's theory was inadequate to explain all that is to be known about the cosmos.

One might wonder if mathematics is adequate to elucidate the nature of Being. Science is the result of observation and mathematics. Observation holds mathematics in check and prevents unbridled speculation. Yet using observation as a check on mathematics limits mathematics to that which is somehow observable. For example theory pointed to the existence of black holes but this theory could not be accepted till there was observable evidence. There now seems to be evidence for the existence of black holes.

Included in mathematics is logic. This does not necessarily point to logical systems per se as it has been shown that mathematics cannot be reduced to traditional logic. But mathematics relies on its own sort of logic that was formed through experience.

If mathematics is tied to experience then how can mathematics begin to understand the infinite? If experience is unlimited when a discovery is made a new field of unexplored wisdom becomes apparent. Can mathematics be infinite? With it's reliance on observation this in fact seems not.

It is true that there are infinite series in mathematics which tell us something about infinity. But like the philosopher Xeno taking a half step repeatedly toward and opposing wall one will never reach the wall. Or when the philosopher Lucretius' warrior throws his spear infinity is that the spear travels on and on.

Einstein calls the problem here as that the universe is infinite but bounded. Like walking on an expanding balloon, one can walk forever without end but if one walks far enough they end up where they began. This seems very different from the way of talking about infinity as being that and more of the finite which composes it. This is very different from finding a boundary of the universe. How can something be infinite and bounded at the same time?

But is Being bound? The examination of Being seems to tell us nothing from observation. The examination of Being seems to depend on unbridled speculation. Kant rails against the excesses of unbridled speculation which excesses tells us little about the real world, the logic of philosophy has seen its excesses as well. It is no accident that the famous dunce Duns Scotus, came up with the most wild and convoluted theory of Being. His philosophy is most certainly the most difficult to read and to understand not because he was a dunce but because through the excesses of wild speculation the result became what was seen to ordinary minds as gibberish.

So is philosophical logic useful at all? An even more important question to ask though is is the world logical? Whether the world is logical or not would render irrelevant the question of whether it is useful.

One basis for modern logic is Aristotle's excluded middle. One thing cannot be both itself and another. If the sun is shining then it is false that the sun is not shining. It cannot be both. There is a correspondence between what one says and the way things are. This idea of the excluded middle is applied to Aristotle's Metaphysics where God is the unmoved mover. This seems almost as nonsensical as his proposition that humans are rational animals. We are either rational or animals, we cannot be both as to be rational is to be human and to be animal is to not be rational. At

119

least this is how humans are traditionally understood. This dichotomy afflicts western philosophy all around, God as the unmoved mover, the relationship between matter and spirit, the relationship between Plato's forms and the world.

So what are we to do? Are we to throw out logic? Are we as lost with philosophical logic as we are about mathematical logic in talking about the nature of Being or infinity?

Sri Aurobindo takes the example of a candles flame and its warmth.

Both are characteristic of the candle. An analogy can be drawn from the flame and its warmth and God the infinite and God the creator. In potentiality comes actuality and actuality depends on potentiality for example talking about the Tao in itself. They cannot be discretely divided. With Aristotle's idea of the unmoved mover we arrive at a point of origin for all that is. Nothing precedes the thing that moves itself. But if the thing that moves itself is that which is the source of all things, that is it is foundational, then how can we call this foundation infinite when what it produces is its creation and therefore does not properly belong to it?

One cannot draw a discrete line between the flame and heat of the candle.

So perhaps Aristotle's foundationalism is flawed. The unmoved mover cannot be that which it produces.

Since Aristotle's position is untenable should we throw logic out? Wouldn't this be throwing the baby out with the bathwater?

Traditional mathematics does not seem to explain the thing of creation. Neither does Aristotle's unmoved mover. But if one takes the position that there can be something that is unmoved that moves something, then that thing can be both the thing that moves and is that which is moved at the same time! This certainly seems to violate the law of the excluded middle which traditional western logic is based on.

But if one talks about the unity of all things there are many implications. From where comes human freedom? How can we have a relationship with God? But the problem is not not having a proper relationship with God, the question rather amounts to what is God at all?

Logic still works on our mundane planet. We can still calculate the distance to Alpha Centauri by using triangles. We cannot use a geometers triangle to understand triangles because ultimately triangles are ideas and we cannot use triangles to understand the all of All.

There is a certain logic though that can be used with Being. Not limited by observation or philosophical logic can tell us much about the nature of Being. Science certainly cannot. But the use of a different philosophical logic then is necessary. We are not troubled by Duns Scotus flawed logic which reduces Being to levels of absurdity being based largely on discrete levels which render the system useless.

The world and infinity exists whether we wish to try and explain it or not. And why not try? With science we always suspend judgment till we get empirical evidence but aren't we curious. And is it ever possible to get observational knowledge of that which is infinite and unbounded? Some may feel that doing this is an idle exercise. Certainly such and understanding would do little for ones life prospects. But then that is the nature of philosophy be it East or West, to think about such things. One can never hold oneself up as a expert or a master or a sovereign. This has been done too often by the flawed metaphysical philosophy of the middle age mystics used to enforce medieval beliefs.

But perhaps such a knowledge can result in a certain peace of mind. Perhaps one can find solace in a world not tied down by worldly problems. Also when looking at the unity of all things one can perhaps find commonalities between all things and one can be more accepting of one's brother more charitable toward the plants and the animals of the world and more tolerant of it's physical beauty.

Philosophy of any stripe cannot tell you about the nature of Being. At least it cannot get you there as the being of Being. But if dogma can excised from one belief systems then one is more amenable to the experience of the divine which composes our true nature and the nature of all. Perhaps then speculative philosophy about the nature of infinite Being without limitation can give us peace and even prepare us for the experience of our true nature as divine beings.

The Supernatural and the Natural

Is the supernatural fundamentally different than the natural? When we talk about the supernatural we think of something that surmounts the natural. The natural is something we can talk about and know, but on the other hand the supernatural is beyond description.

The natural we perceive but the supernatural we do not perceive. How are they different? The natural is composed of the finite. We can know the natural because of its being perceptible and transient.

The supernatural on the other hand is composed of the infinite. We cannot sense the supernatural because the infinite is not perceptible and is intransient.

Our senses are limited. In order to perceive that which is perceived must be distinguished from what it is not. Also what is perceived must be distinguished from what it may become. The myriad generation of variation at play in the natural world is marked by transience and corruptibility.

But one that perceives the variability of the finite knows the characteristics of the natural. One who knows the invariability of the infinite knows the characteristics of the supernatural but knows this not through perception but through consciousness.

When one thinks of the finite one thinks of that which is limited unlike the infinite. When one thinks of the infinite one thinks of that which is unlimited unlike the finite.

But both the finite and the infinite depend on each other. The finite is limited and the infinite is not. The finite and the infinite are inexorably tied together.

Something that is limited is corruptible while that which is unlimited is not.

123

Perception can only know that which is limited because only the limited is subject to change and therefore varies from everything else, while the infinite cannot be perceived because it is unlimited and therefore knows no variation or weakness or strength or dissolution or decay or growth and on ad infinitum and therefore is not perceptible.

Traditional Hinduism says life is illusion. Sri Aurobindo says this in fact is not true. Maya or ignorance is the result of a lack of consciousness. We cannot penetrate the infinite with perception because perception depends on the finite and is finite itself and is therefore limited in itself. Perception is ultimately the result of spiritual and therefore biological evolution.

But through consciousness viz a viz experience one can penetrate this narrowing of experience brought about by perception and increase ones God consciousness (i.e., the infinite).

The finite and the infinite are not fundamentally different. One cannot exist without the other. But as explained before the finite is the realm of perception and the infinite can only be known through consciousness that which is fundamentally ourselves.

Therefore though it seems that the supernatural and the natural are fundamentally different they really are not, but seem to be so because they each can only be known in their own way.

Nature and the Elemental: A Study on the Finite and the Infinite

Western philosophy has always had a tension when trying to explain the finite and the infinite. If something is finite then it cannot be infinite because it is limited in number. Even if you added all the finite things up they would still be finite because they would be limited in number. Where does infinity come in?

The problem arises as to how can things be ultimately limited in nature? When Lucretius talks about throwing a spear in space if things are not limited then the spear will go on and on to infinity. But as the spear transits space it can be measured and therefore will continue for an infinite amount of time so as never to reach infinity. So infinite space seems to encompass infinite time.

But as Einstein stated there is no time. But there is change. Time is used as a useful way of thinking about change. But change is not uniform. As we now know a snail may move a few inches and hour, while at the same time light traverses worlds and in principle both can approach infinity. With universal expansion the measure of time becomes useless as expansion approaches infinity.

But the finite and the infinite are not really different. The infinite depends on the finite and the finite depends on the infinite similarly as large includes small and peace includes war.

Finite is no more knowable than the infinite. Just as something cannot be understood reasonably as being infinite, neither can something be considered finite. If the universe is infinite which it seems it must it must be made up of finite things otherwise how would we exist? Yet the infinite seems to be more than the sum of the finite.

Contrariwise the finite cannot be really known either. As the infinite is made up of the finite (and yet is more than the sum of its parts) the finite must be made up of the infinite. Why? Just as the

125

infinite is composed of the finite, the finite is composed of the infinite. When we examine the finite for example a statue of Lucretius we can examine the hand of the human figure, then the finger, and then it's finger nail, and then its essential marble essence. We can even take this forward as we know in modern day science that marble has a molecular structure, an atomic structure and so on and so on. Just as the infinite is composed of the finite (and more so), the finite is composed of the infinite (and more so). It seems then that all things are part and parcel of the infinite and the finite.

So where do humans dwell? Humans physically are finite. This finiticity is what makes it knowable. For us to know something it must be knowable. Perception depends on the finite, but this does not remove from aggregation with the infinite or its disintegration with forever infinite smallness.

When talking about matter and spirit matter is only important to consider if it is knowable and therefore it must be finite. As has been claimed here before something cannot be infinite and finite in the same element. The nature of something finite is particular to the elemental nature involved and is not generalizable to the finite in general. This is how a finite element cannot be both finite and yet has a generalized nature (the infinite) at the same time.

The mistake comes when thinking about the finite as having a nature in only itself. Spirit (e.g., as nature) and matter (e.g., an element) are exclusively delineated.

Yet the finite cannot have a generalized nature and the infinite cannot have an elemental nature; this conflicts with the nature of elements composing that which is infinitely large and the finite composed of elements that which are infinitely small.

The basic problem with the antinomy is that all things are infinite in nature but can only be understood in a finite manner. As the idealists show the nature of our perception depends on our sensory apparatus. A bee's eye perceives light very differently from the way humans perceive it although the light has not changed. It is all things to all sentient beings. The ways of understanding something is only limited by the nature of the perceptible organ. There are no limits on the thing being perceived except only in the act of being perceived. So not only is it true that things can only be known if they are finite the thing known must be infinite as the possible ways of it being known are infinite.

So describing something as finite gets the cart before the horse. We understand things as being finite only because this is the nature of perception. Perception in principle is not limited but the way things are perceived in the individual perceiving thing are. Without this distinction between perception and the thing perceived it would be clear to see that nothing is limited and is rather the perceptual consequence of consciousness. With self-identity we can have knowledge but these perceptible things do not make ourselves simply a nature unto ourselves.

Consciousness evolving in life results in the spirit coming to know itself. How can something be anything at all if it cannot know itself? This is how the infinite becomes finite and the finite becomes infinite by one knowing ones self by cultivating consciousness. While we may have knowledge of the finite through our perceptual apparatus we can know both the finite and the infinite through consciousness.

Consciousnessess then renders the concept of finiticity as obsolete. The spear when thrown into space must travel forever because simply this must be so because how can it be bounded? Like a tree, one may enjoy the fragrance of its flowers but only one fully conscious can realize the salubrious effect of eating its fruit.

The Base of Dogma

Where do the ideas for Yoga Philosopher come from? They come from a fundamental or foundational base or dogma.

Some may disagree with my ideas, but rather than the medievals who based their beliefs on a fundamental issue (the transcendence of God and the immanent world), I take the position that all things are one perhaps not a homogenous whole or an amorphous entity but rather simply recognizing the fact that one knows intuitively that it is not reasonable to think that there is a supramundane world that houses as is often thought an anthropomorphic God.

The problem is not simply with the anthropomorphic character of God but that this sort of dualism which is hypostasized between the mundane and the supramundane has been a problem throughout history and it seems that it will never be solved and in fact is not solvable. One only needs to look at Descartes Mind/Body problem, which the question is asked how an immaterial substance (e.g., the mind) can affect a material substance (e.g., the body).

Since these two things are fundamentally different they cannot in fact interface and this too is a problem that seems will never be solved. So dualism aside from its practical epistemological applications cannot be defended metaphysically. One can see clearly that when one talks about the supernatural they are talking about something that seems to be beyond understanding rather than something that is fundamentally different from our world of existence.

If you dissolve the distinction better matter and spirit, the supramental God and mundane world, this problem disappears in a rather unique application of Occam's razor. It seems that finding that all is spirit or all is God is a position that makes sense. This is the great contribution of Aurobindo's thought. This book falls from this dogmatic foundation. But the belief in the nature of God being All does not depend on faith or simply faith alone but comes from what seems to be the only reasonable way of describing the world. The useful thing about this position is that it can be reconciled with the scientific world view but this view departs from the scientific world view in a fundamental way.

This difference is that science draws the line on what can empirically be tested, yet in fact one can talk about things ex cathedra based on a sort of philosophical speculation. Science might argue strongly this position because it takes things beyond the empirical. Yet of course there are infinite tools in mathematics. Scientists like the Buddhists may not talk about the nature of God or as in Hinduism the infinite but this does not show that such a metaphysics in some form cannot be talked about but simply that to talk about it is not "practical".

What then is the importance of this position? Well philosophy has usually not been thought of as being practical and this position on its own seems to be no different. But there are attitudinal and political ramifications for the world by taking the only logical position of God being All.

Just suffice it to say then that Oneness of God is the basis of this books dogma, and the reason again it is taken is because dualism if history is any judge is not a viable position at least metaphysically, and therefore the oneness of all seems to be the only position that can be used to make any sort of sense.

Thus is the base of my dogma.

Why is a New Metaphysical Determination Important in Western Philosophical Thought?

Why is a new metaphysical determination important in western philosophical thought? Western scientific thought like Buddhism ignores Vedantic metaphysics. Rather than having an organizing principle such as Brahman or the All speculation about such things is ignored and even dismissed.

Western scientific thought generally claims that metaphysical constructs are useless. Oftentimes the appeal to Occam's razor appears to show that a metaphysical construct is not useful to the scientific task at hand and should be excised. An example here is when one turns on the lights:

1. One flips the switch 2. The metaphysical fairies travel through the electrical line 3. Then these fairies cause the illumination of the lights.

The point here is that there is no reason to posit a metaphysical component of an otherwise natural phenomenon. Science after all is objective and dismisses out of hand any sort of "supernatural" impulses.

But the thing that is often ignored is that in fact there is a way of understanding the world that science uses which stands over and above simply its epistemological (e.g., ways of knowing) manifestations. It cannot be denied that epistemologically science has no equal. But science does not recognize that it too is bound to certain dogma in order to apply its epistemological theories.

As stated many times scientific methods borrow on Descartes epistemological theories. Descartes project is to show that perception is reliable. He does this by positing the cogito, that there is the thing that thinks and the thinking thing (e.g., the mind and the body). This famous declaration has made western science unparalleled in world thought.

Coming out of this Descartean perspective is an objectification of the world. When a scientist conducts an experiment the mind of the scientist is an active creative force which examines the seemingly inert environment. Anything that is not human is relegated to inert matter. Even "animals" are not thought by many to possess the creative impulse that is available only to humans. This orientation is a not so subtle reflection of Descartes postulate of the creative mind and obtuse matter.

One doesn't need to go much further to realize that in fact the orientation of mind and body according to Descartes has its own roots in western religion. Science would be unlikely to admit this but one simply needs to look at the evidence. In western religion we have the Creator and the created. We have the Divine mind and we have "his" creation the universe. He then put the world in service of his most favored creation "Man".

One thing that is interesting to note is that the western Holy Bible introduces God at the point of inception of the world. An explanation is never given for the existence of God, and it seems clear that such a description at least from a religious viewpoint is not necessary. It is God after all, God is beyond any defect and therefore a discussion of origin of God is not necessary.

Nevertheless this omnipresence of God summarily being thrust upon us through science stands as a problem demonstrated by western ancient philosophy that Aristotle tries to conquer with his presentation of the unmoved mover. This problem in a nutshell is how can a thing both move and move itself and still be a unitary entity. This problem is exacerbated by the birth of Christ which theologians attempted to explain through the concept of the trinity. Attempts to bridge this schism resulted in the lore of angels which were messengers between God and Man. Humans, unlike other parts of nature possessed a soul which through God enabled one to think freely, creatively and justly.

After the death of the body the soul would travel to be reunited with God or would be condemned to eternal damnation. But the relation of the soul to the body is as difficult to explain as is the relationship between Descartes' mind and body or even and perhaps because of the schism between God and his creation.

But aside from the viability of such an epistemological system exemplified in Descartes' "Meditations" there are problems throughout western scientific as well as religious and philosophical thought in the dynamism of the creator and the created, and the mind and body from a metaphysical perspective (i.e., looking at it as a problem in theorizing about metaphysics).

But not only is this a theoretical problem, but it is also a practical problem as well. Rather than placing ourselves as equal participants in the world standing alongside plants, animals, and the material and spiritual, we find ourselves as has been the inclination through western human weltanschauung to see ourselves as the center of the universe as well as the center of all creativity and intelligence being the arbiters of morality and integrity. This results from our religious (ostensibly) heritage. But as often happens with dogma our foundational beliefs are taken for granted and never questioned.

Plainly stated then there is in fact a metaphysical perspective which goes unstated in scientific thought that "Westerners" are wedded to.

The concept of an All does not run contrary to western religious and philosophical tradition which has raised the creator God as being supremely important. If God is truly omnipotent then the viability of a God that can be all and is all does not conflict specifically with the singular concept of a creator God.

Aside from this being an important issue from a religious and philosophical perspective it is important as well practically. A theory of a God of All resolves the mind/body problem in Descartes system simply eliminating this distinction using Occam's razor.

But in addition to solving this basic metaphysical problem taking the perspective of a God that dwells everywhere not unlike the western assertion of divine omnipresence one can see not only the divineness but the Godliness of all of God creations. From a more generous religious perspective we can talk about God the creator as well as God the omnipresent and omniscient. This is important not only to resolve contradictions in science, theology and philosophy but also our attitude toward the natural world.

While it may be true that we can't justify bending our philosophical leanings just to serve utility I claim we have not done so and I am trying to make clear this relationship between environmental degradation and our way of looking at the world with it's poverty of environmental integrity which stems from our own limited but not flawed way of looking at the natural world.

Largely the reason for environmental degradation is the result of our view of nature as being a dead and inert substance subject to our free dominance and manipulation. If we can recognize how the traditional western philosophical tradition is limited we can clearly see how a metaphysical perspective informs our attitudes toward ourselves and the world. Without seeing the world as being commissurate with ourselves we cannot give it equal treatment.

It may be because of our acclimation to our accepted western dogma that we may not be unwilling to change. But when we look at the world around us it is easy to see that things do not seem to be going right. Why not take a more cosmopolitan view and right the errors of the past so that we may ensure the integrity of the future theologically, philosophically and environmentally. In doing this we will be doing service to systems of belief in philosophy and environmental and physical sciences always reaffirming the omnipotence of God.

Is the Infinite Conceivable?

It seems clear that the cosmos cannot be limited in any way. For if there was at some point limitation then that limitation itself would be necessarily unlimited. If the universe came to an abrupt wall, say for an example a wall of granite then this wall of granite would be as thick as necessary to either delineate another parallel cosmos or an infinite thickness of granite. Space itself does not delimit in itself the cosmos and neither does a physical structure. So it seems that a finite universe is inconceivable.

Modus Tollens can be used here.

If P then Q

~Q Therefore ~P

The argument goes if the universe is finite then there must be some limit There is no limit (e.g., a limit is not conceivable) Therefore the universe is infinite (not finite)
So if a finite cosmos is inconceivable then the cosmos must be infinite.
If something is conceivable then it is possible. If something is not conceivable then it is not possible. Take for example square circles or violet blues which are inconceivable and therefore not possible.
It seems that human rationality can be relied on, for if it cannot then what can we rely on? We would be a like a ship at sea without a rudder approaching the eye of a hurricane.
But it seems clear that we do survive so it is clear that in the very least our cognitions are useful and to be useful they must tell us basic things about the world.

134

Take for example the strides made in empirical science which uses induction generalizing from a specific number of instances to support a hypothesis or law.

So not only are our perceptions reliable and our generalizations about cognitions seem to be based largely on our perceptions that being a rational creature we are able to come up with apt postulates about the nature of the world, the universe and the cosmos.

But is the infinite really conceivable? Could space and matter just go on and on and on? There seems to be no contradiction in principle. We could not use a reductio ad absurdum to rule out the idea of an infinite cosmos.

But can we imagine an infinite space? Probably not. Might not even be a good idea to try.

If one accepts that the cosmos is infinite then it is hard to find a place for us in it. If things get infinitely large as well as infinitely small then how do we account for our present existence in the world? We are born, live and die. We get married, have children, and maybe have grandchildren and then give up the ghost as is often said. What is our point of reference?

We are inclined to ask why. This impulse results in us positing a transcendental being. Certainly we must have some reason for being here. What meaning could life have if we are simply a parcel in infinity? Certainly it is hoped someone somewhere who matters cares for us.

It certainly is a lonely universe. But exist we do and exist we must. And our existence is the crux of the mystery.

Problems With the Atheist's Position

Atheists deny vehemently the existence of God. Usually when the atheist thinks of God they are thinking of the anthropomorphic God of the Abrahamic tradition. The idea of God as comprising everything there is would not run counter to the atheist's position as long as there was not more to it. It would be a matter of definition.

Certainly though the atheist is resistant to using the word God. This is largely because God in the Abrahamic tradition has been used to justify all sorts of wickedness. Aside from this another reason would be the more analytical that one need not talk about what one cannot know. That is this objection is to talking about God as a mystical entity. If it is not known and therefore cannot be talked about then it is nothing but nonsense according to the atheist.

I've often wondered whether this is a metaphorical way of looking at all there is or rather that it is an epistemological position (e.g., theory of knowledge)? If it were metaphorical then it would be a rejection of that which is not known but may someday be known; but to the atheists if it is unknown now they assert there is no point in talking about it. While this position borders on the Agnostic position the positing of God is rejected; rather than one suspending judgment as is so in the agnostic's case.

On the other hand if it is an epistemological position that since something cannot be known then it is not something that we can have knowledge of and therefore must reject it. The epistemological position is the primary position for the atheist when the atheist thinks about God. To say God exists is meaningless if we don't have a way of understanding God. This seems to follow from the epistemological positions of science (e.g., in empiricism).

Let us deal with the epistemological position because this is a position that can be examined using Jnana Yoga.

While the epistemological position is a very strong argument against positing a God, there is much confusion in principle by the atheist when assuming that God always refers to a transcendent anthropomorphic deity which thinks and in turn judges us. It seems that the atheist tends to be a western phenomenon. Atheists often find themselves wedded to the scientific tradition rooted in skepticism. This skepticism has its roots in the works of Descartes and even goes back to the Ancient Greeks as shown by Sextus Empiricus. But talking about God as a transcendent being is not the only way of talking about God.

One might ask the atheist if they would accept the proposition that God is nature. This would probably seem redundant to the atheist which is why talk about God at all but rather simply talk about nature. The atheist might reason that since God has no intelligence and is therefore unable to make judgments, then why talk about God at all when one talks about nature? But once again this results from a misunderstanding about how we can talk about God.

Surely to everyone nature is a mystery. We can do experiments, map out equations, but the final constant cannot be found. Complexity abounds.

If a scientist was able to come to the "final" answer then the scientist would be larger than that answer. But this seems counter-intuitive in our infinite universe.

The search by the atheist for God then rests with a scientistic position that all can be known at least in principle. But how can that be if we cannot even tell what is going to happen tomorrow?

It seems that the unknown will never have its veil removed. Weathermen can make predictions, eclipses can be charted but whether you oversleep the next morning and are late for work can

137

never be known. There is always the unknown and the unknowable.

But is this an argument for God? Perhaps, but perhaps not. But we do know that everything may not be known (e.g., the metaphorical position) and even the epistemological position as well that we cannot know the unknowable (e.g., the mystical) and therefore is meaningless and yet it seems clear that things do and will always be unknowable (i.e., the infinite). If we accept this then we cannot rule out the unknowable as God, or in nature or rather God as nature in its infinite manifestations. Yet this does not rule out other ways of knowing God as well.

A Justification For My Work

Some may wonder why I have written this book.

When living ones life one wants to have a legacy. I have no children, no fortune. But I hope to leave something to the world that may be useful. It troubles me the things that are going on in the world. The USA exerts its influence throughout the world based on violence.

Sometimes I'm not sure whether this is the way things naturally are human nature based on violence or whether this is a particular American invention. I think to answer this one needs to look at history. There is ample evidence to demonstrate that some cultures have lived in peace but have been supplanted by the more violent cultures.

To put things another way is human behavior especially United State's weltanschauung typical of the human species at large or is it just part of United States culture?

An even more important question is is violent behavior part of our genetic endowment or is it part of social conditioning? This is an important question. The world has reached a threshold where we find ourselves facing each other with ever more violent weapons. Was this outcome necessary that is is this outcome a part of our human nature? Or is this part of our teachings?

We find ourselves at every turn having this ideology of force and violence used against us. As children we are called sissies or even "fags" if we show any compassion for our fellow human beings.

But history is notable for relatively peaceful attitudes outlooks and behaviors toward the world. A good example are the Buddhists or some US Indigenous nations.

Yet in the US such an attitude is looked at as being soft and in some cases when violence is used against such peaceful inhabitants this is looked upon as being justified a sort of Darwinism where the conquering people are doing the human species a service. Of course such things were not what Darwin intended at all
Now the world is surrounded by saber rattling nations vowing "justice".

Certainly if this is the makeup of the human species then this must be part of our genetic endowment. But if one considers the matter one finds that those nations that do not pursue war and do not produce weapons fall easy prey to those that have these sinister weapons. With the attitude of pillage and plunder these peaceful people are overthrown and destroyed.

Yet the question is is this peaceful nature the "natural" outcome of human behavior. In other words is this behavior some part of our genetic endowment, or is it the case now that the former "peaceful" members of the world are eliminated perhaps eliminating this gene?

If one takes the twisted Darwinistic perspective promoted by the violent peoples of the world then one finds that while violent behavior may have been justified at some point in our history that is from an egoistic perspective that this is not the case now, as many nations possess weapons which we can use to annihilate each other.

So if the human species is determined by our genes then we are about to jump off the cliff like lemmings to perish from our own weapons as in science fiction where humans are overthrown by robots their own invention which comes to destroy them.
First of all we must decide if there is some sort of "violence" gene. Secondly the question is is there a corresponding "peace" gene. Thirdly has the peace gene been eliminated from the genome by the violence prone peoples of the world?

140

Finally if the foregoing is not true then is human behavior not determined by our genetic endowment but is rather a learned behavior, then there is hope for humankind. Otherwise it seems all is lost.

It's hard to know if this aspect of human behavior is genetic or learned. Nevertheless examining racism it is clear that the genetic endowment between humans varies little. There is no characteristic except for example skin color or our hair characteristics that makes us different intrinsically as human beings. In other words these differences are inconsequential and to assert that these characteristics are a significant difference amounts to bias and in some cases racism.

If one needs more evidence for this then one only needs to trace blood types through human groups to discover that there is no "genetic" characteristic that differentiates humans essentially according to this. So it seems unlikely that we are predetermined to exhibit violent behavior to other humans, or that this supposed peaceful "gene" has been wiped out in the act of Social Darwinism.

Or if it is in fact the case that there is a gene that determines human behavior especially violent behavior toward other humans then there is a gene for peaceful peoples in our past and that even peoples that are peaceful that exist today. So it is the case or at least it may be hoped that it is the case that the human species have the ability to coexist with other peoples of the world without the necessity of destroying them if this peaceful gene can be preserved.

So perhaps then we should rejoice there is hope!

But perhaps there is not any hope at all. That even if this behavior is not part of our essence but rather part of the learned experience that people can be brought to realize their own self interest. Certainly the human species must be saved!

But when one realizes that we are simply the result of the primordial chain of life, that as we came into existence as a specie, too we certainly will perish or at least become something uniquely different from today. Perhaps our influence will be felt for millions of years as the birds have in which many feel they are descendents of the dinosaurs.

But is it important for the human species to continue to exist? What if we were to become extinct as other species eventually do? Does nature care? Does God care if we exist?

If you take the religious perspective we are the creation of God in God's image. Our existence is valuable as an extension of God's creation and in a sense all are chosen by God. As with Aristotle where the planets made circles around the earth or Ptolemy where the planets too revolved around the earth or Copernicus where the solar system was heliocentric but our solar system still was at the center of all. And with Einstein we find that at every point in space that point is the center in reference to itself as all things are.

This vanity of the human species as being in some sense divine in nature is quickly being wiped out by science as it becomes clear that we are just another species in the primordial chain of being that began with the Big Bang and subsequently is acting out of dynamism of the hydrogen atom.

So does the universe or "God" care about us as a species? Are we favored in any way by the expanse of all in which we live? Or are we simply the unfolding of an infinite chain of being which continues on and on.

Not only is the question about whether or not we are simply a part of the cosmic order that cares nothing about us, but rather should we care whether the universe cares about us or even should we care about ourselves?

If we blow ourselves up does the earth care? If we irradiate the planet does the planet care? It seems not. Should we care? Are we important enough to preserve for anything at all? If not it doesn't matter what kind of wholesale slaughter takes place what sort of genocide occurs? It seems that this ultimately is the decision of the primordial chain of being. Like a bouncing ball if one kicks it it moves in a certain direction determined by the physical properties of kinesis.

So as we are barreling down the path of life if we are determined by our "violent" genes the question is not only can we change it but is it worth changing?

The question becomes important that are we really free? If we are not free this question is important in many respects. If we are not free then we cannot change the path that humans are transversing and also if we are determined like an insane man cannot be found culpable of a crime we cannot talk about the ethical proscriptions about whether we are "worth" saving.

So if we have this violent gene or not, it matters not if we are not free. So should we find freedom? Or must we find it? It seems we must grasp at freedom out of the same egoistic desire which dooms us down this primordial chain of being. We should ask not why we should have freedom but rather does freedom exist? Otherwise what's the point?

We should not decide this question out of a desire to justify our own existence, to do so would skew the question that is if we are matter following certain universal laws or that we are in fact free thinking beings.

But this brings us back to our original question. Are we determined and do we have a violent gene or not? Are we destined to bring about our own extinction or can the world be saved and also are we worth saving?

If we can in fact save ourselves we must be free to do so. And if we are free to do so then it seems we do have moral worth. So if we can save ourselves then we have moral worth.

It is my belief that the human specie is worth saving. It is also my belief that it is possible to save it. And if we are free then we are in fact able to act morally. If we are able to act morally then we can end violence against our brothers and sisters. In fact we must do that. Otherwise we cannot save ourselves and even more importantly we are not worth saving and therefore are not moral beings.

If we are free thinking this then makes us human endowed with this gift of creation by God or the infinite. If we are able to save ourselves it seems then we are worth saving otherwise it matters not our extinction and it seems nothing has been lost.

Following then in my work includes a justification for the positing of human freedom and an importance for our being in the world. A justification for our existence is in the infinite universe in this wide expanse where we would be easily lost in its enormity.

In order to change we must believe in something otherwise the outcome matters not. Whether this is science, or God, or the Infinite this belief enables us to fulfill what seems to be our destiny. That destiny is to survive and flourish, to reproduce and change to adapt as the world changes, to prevail throughout the mountains and fissures of the world as they present themselves.

To believe presupposes freedom and to be free justifies our existence and our importance. To be free enables us to join hands and face the future together not moving toward extinction or to be swept off the world by a divine hand but rather to find our place in the cosmos among the suns and planets and the other solar systems and stars and perhaps other species of distant worlds crying out for meaning. To be free implies our ability to survive. This ability to survive proves our moral integrity. This is human dignity.
Lets then stand firmly on the earth and affirm our existence for to do not is for naught.

The Myth of Purity

Because of the valuing of the spiritual over the physical the physical is often looked at as being impure. This belief harkens back to Plato's forms of Beauty, Justice, and so on which were pure in nature. In making a distinction between the spiritual perfection and physical corruption one is led to value the spiritual over the physical. But a distinction cannot really be made between "spirit" and "body." This is because the common idea of that which is body and that which is spirit is fundamentally different and therefore cannot reside in the human form together. People are taught to be God like which is to be perfect in nature. But of course human nature has another idea. I remember my mother washing out my mouth with soap to impress upon me that I must be pure in speech as a part of spirit.

It is interesting to note that often the people that claim to be the most spiritual (e.g., that is pure in nature) tend to turn out as the most "corrupt". It seems that one who tries to deny their human nature may fall even more bound to it. Oftentimes people attempt to control their nature which is especially troubling to them and they therefore may have an even larger problem with sensuality than most others.

Purity implies our divine nature. Many feel if they were not so impure and were not bound to the 7 deadly sins (pride, avarice, envy, wrath, lust, gluttony and sloth) which result from our physical sinful nature then we could be united with the divine, either in this life or in the hereafter. When one commits sin this displeases God according to some.

It seems clear that it is fruitless to try to oppose our "sinful" nature. It seems we can never hope to achieve perfection. But if you don't posit the spiritual as being fundamentally different from

145

the physical one comes to realize that we are already perfect and therefore are not capable of sin contrary to what the puritans claim.

This is not meant to be encouragement for one to descend into some heinous criminal spree but rather to recognize that we contain a nature that is both physical and filled with life. As a species we are at this point the most adept at survival. We don't achieve this by being somehow basically flawed. We would have been eliminated from the gene pool long ago. The emphasis on purity creates a feeling of guilt in the individual because one is never never able to completely defy ones own nature.

It is better to not make the rapt distinction between body and spirit and recognize that in our spiritual being we are divine. At the very least we are God's creation which makes us divine; at the most we are the divinity itself. The sin comes in by looking at ourselves as being separate from God when in fact our nature is identical with God itself or as God's creation. If we realized we were divine then we would know that we need not feel guilty about our human nature and would not find the need to grasp at purity.

Nevertheless being tightly bound to the senses roots one in the physicality of existence and can limit our understanding of our divine nature. It is the attachment to the senses according to the Buddha that causes suffering. This attachment to the senses should not be avoided because it makes us impure, but rather because it prevents us being united with God in our own self or in God beyond. There is no evil judgment of you by God in this fact no malice toward you if you dwell in the senses, but you will never realize your true nature as being divine and this is a terrible shame, that is it's too bad it can't be otherwise.

This bounding to the senses can result in a sort of slavery to one's nature and this results in pain. One needs to avoid this bondage not because it is sinful but because one needs to be free. This can be achieved through consciousness, that is God consciousness. There is no evil in this formulation unless evil means that one is acting in a manner that separates them from the bliss of God realization. To look down on someone or to persecute them because of their bondage to the senses is both inhumane and callous. Why not instead help them realize their own divinity and they then can overcome their own helplessness and bondage.

There is no purity unless you accept that we are pure in body and spirit. Making the erroneous distinction between body and spirit is the only justification used to advance the cause of purity. Only by recognizing our helplessness can we truly become free. This surrender helps one get a glimpse of ones Godly nature and forces this sickness out. Self acceptance is the key. This is the first step in which one can begin to be free of the bondage of the senses and to realize their own divine nature. One cannot change the self of oneself. This is like trying to raise a sack of garbage while standing on top of it. When you grasp at purity you act out of blindness to the true nature of self and that nature is to be fully conscious and free.

The Arrogance of Humans

We all have those wonderful brains. Our brains separate us from the less fortunate animals or so we claim.

Since we dominate the earth we think that we are better than the earth. We have overrun the planet like a nest of roaches out of control. We pollute the planet, destroy the animals, kill the plants and overall are turning the earth into a desolate sphere.

We with our souls, we are the only ones favored by God. Others are just here to serve us.

With our private property everything is a possession. Its only value is the value it is to us. And once we no longer find it valuable we discard it as trash.

And we hear a lot of talk about the sanctity of life. As the deceased comedian George Carlin states in one of his routines as paraphrased, "it's interesting that those that talk about the sanctity of life are only the living. The dead have no part and it is really meaningless." I mean we are all going to die someday.

Yet we strive to extend life through good health. But who can argue against good health? One might have liposuction to remove the fat, a face lift to remove that second chin. But what is it for? We have a heaven above to save us. We are going to live forever!, live in heaven with God, or burn in damnation till eternity. But live on we must.

But when you look at the world nothing lives long.

While the streams turn to rivers, the river banks turn to valleys and finally canyons; then tectonic forces raise it up again.

And the sun revolves around the earth, or nowadays it's the earth that revolves around the sun.

We are even on the periphery of the milky way galaxy spinning.

And of course we are not at the middle of the infinite universe either.

148

Such vanity in us humans.

Such arrogance.

What is the Purpose of Spirituality and Religion?

Well the first thing that occurs to me is that if we ask what is the purpose of spirituality or religion that religion or spirituality is something we do to achieve something rather than religion or spirituality being an expression of the most heartfelt feeling of a people.

I draw a sharp distinction between spirituality and religion. Religion implies some dogma that must be accepted in order to be an adherent of that belief. Spirituality can mean the same thing to some people but for me it refers to the ideal, the beautiful, an expression of altruistic love.

To be spiritual one does not adhere to dogmatic principles which make a religion "different" from other beliefs. The "spirit" can be the animating force which drives us that unites us that delivers us in a different sense than what the bible talks about in the atonement.

I've found that people think that spirit is something particular to humans and this sets us apart from the "animals". For some spirit implies the soul so that when someone has the spirit they can go to heaven or hell. To some when we have spirit it is because God breaths into us life. But spirit is not something that only humans possess. Spirit is everything and nothing. It is the composite of existence. Not only do humans possess spirit but all life has spirit.

In this sense all is the creation of God, the eternal spirit has breathed spirit into all, all is God's creation be it Humans, "animals" plants, rocks, rivers, streams and perhaps even the space that divides them. So if spirit is to have a "purpose" at all it can be that it instills respect in us for all things, that we come from all things and one day we will all return to that from which we have come.

So not only is it to "use" spirituality to recognize God's will in ourselves but the world too. We can have a unity with the world and the spirit can serve us as we commune with the world. The isolation that comes about when we believe that we are the only thing that comprises spirit and has value while all else is inconsequential matter results in not only a separation from the world but a denial of ourselves. It is important to love not only ourselves as unique but to extend that love to others and the world as a whole.

A last word on religion is that true religion comes about from the beautiful teachings of inspired beings be it Jesus, the Buddha, Krishna, Mohammad. These spiritual beings imparted much wisdom and brought us to a higher level of consciousness.

These teachings then are not so different from the spiritualism which we embrace as we embrace the divine. But humans so often want to claim that they speak for these divine beings rather than to let the words of these enlightened avatars speak for themselves.

The Humility of a Yogi

Yogi's are humbles beings. In the same way also are Buddhists. Taking respite in spirit is the action of the enlightened in harmonious times. But the Yogi and Buddhist are responsible for the welfare of the people. When people are threatened then the Yogi must act. This does not happen through violence. But also this does not occur though self-denial.

Action is a natural action. Yogis after all are humans and gods, at least in the respect that we are all gods. Only those that are confused about their true nature can act contrary to the will of the people. And the will of the people in its primitive state follows the action of what is natural. When I say primitive I mean a spirit unclouded by coercion, appeals to greed and vanity absent self-interest which is the spirit of humankind.

When those that are so clouded in their thinking act to destroy those that want only peace then the people must take action but never violent action. Violent action leads to hatred and then it is a fair fight with a determined outcome where either side or both lose.

It is not necessary for a Yogi to escape the world. The Yogi lives in the world and is part of it like anyone else. To deny ones attachment to the physicality of all that exists is to deny the vessel that carries the spirit. For without the vessel the spirit would be without a home. Without a home the spirit would metaphorically at least linger and waft away.

The proper place for the spirit is in its earthly vessel. It might even be said that without the identity of spirit with matter spirit could not exist and this identity can only come about by a separation of spirit from itself and this dictates a physical structure. Human nature is spirit coming to know itself.

So deeply rooted in the world as vanguards of the spirit one must move to act when other spiritual (physical) beings entreat.

Evil cannot be beat by its own tools. Resistance depends on all remaining rooted in the commonality of all the spirit of all. Only then can humankind act against evil, evil meaning ones separation from their own godly nature. For if the evil people kill us all then nothing is lost because they shall perish too. This is their karma.

To act against all is as one cuts off their hand which they use to procure their food. It is in the interest of the evil ones to preserve that which cares for them and those that have not preserve those that have. Such is the nature of the capital based system.

Humility can sometimes result in false consciousness. This humility is not based on resentment. It is not even really humility, but it appears to be even though this is the natural action of the spirit. For the spirit seeks to harm none and is only interested in the play of satisfactions especially with others. Only through acting is one lost. But when one finds a way to be that which serves as a channel for the spirit and the heralder of the coming age of enlightenment can satisfaction rule the day.

The Randomness

There is physicality but also there is freedom, or at least there seems to be. Physicality is determinant while spirituality is undetermined or so it seems.

Descartes mind body problem is irreconcilable but there is something called mind and something called body.

Science too talks about matter and mind but in a different manner. The mind of humankind according to science does not rely on the spirit but is a God unto itself. In this respect the scientist, at least some, consider themselves Gods as they manipulate nature applying technology. It is well known that scientists are an atheistic or agnostic bunch at least more so than the population at large. Yet in a sense scientists are God's. Their enlightened Being enables them through mathematics to describe the variation in the universe.

But ultimately science rests on the Descartean mind body problem where metaphysics is ignored and epistemology reins supreme. But of course epistemology is a way of understanding but tells us nothing directly about the nature of things and what drives these things. Epistemology relies on observation and therefore can only be inductive as Hume proved. But are there things that are necessary? This is the crux of a major problem. There seems to be no evidence that there are necessary things so the knowledge we claim to have rests on an uncertain foundation. The scientist can claim to know nothing with certainty. Even scientific laws are not etched in stone and can be changed by contravening evidence. So we have the uncertainty of knowledge and the necessity of physical structure. Gravitational laws dictate that a stone dropped from a cliff will fall at a certain rate but we cannot know this from our futile observations. The physicality of the stuff of being has an atomic structure, obeys physical laws, changes, and decays and is changed again. These facts may be known with a high degree of probability but one cannot be certain. While this probability may be reassuring, the Ptolemaic universe differed markedly from the Copernican. And the Copernican was not adequate for Galileo or Newton.

The flat landers ruled the world for a long time, but the great mariners proved the world was round, but now we know that the world is not simply round but oval. Round and round the world turns as it passes through the universe which twirls through the cosmos. All determined by physical laws that are never fully understood.

Einstein claimed he had the final word on the structure of space-time but quantum mechanics defeated him. So not only can we not depend on observation, but we cannot depend on mathematics either. For human abstraction always knows limits. The things that rule the universe cannot be known or understood as they are. This is what is called sometimes the infinite. But why is this? Is there a foundation or not?

Take the mind and the body, this intractable problem. Descartes considers the mind to be free, and this determines the nature of observation. But how can this mind interact with the physical body which is physically determined? Where does freedom end and determinism begin? This is a problem that the mighty Kant wrestled with inconclusively. Can something be determined and at the same time be free? This is certainly counter-intuitive.

So induction is inexact and deduction is incomplete. So what is one to do? There is the randomness, the randomness of all things. This randomness determines the endless changes that occur in evolution. This randomness ceases to find order in prime numbers. The value of Pythagoras' Pi has not been determined in spite of the most powerful computers. Is it that there is no foundation? If not then there is an infinite regress or a circular regress which explains nothing. But if we find a foundation how can we understand it? If there is a determinant foundation then we are reduced to unthinking automatons.

But randomness seems to be both foundational and unfounded at the same time perhaps. The outcome of change can never be determined. Whether things are evolving or devolving or go in cycles of each cannot be determined and this sort of conception may be incorrect and useless and simply a anthropocentric value judgment. It is clear talking about evolution or devolution, utopia or dystopia owes nothing to that which relies on randomness.

Can we understand God in randomness? Randomness knows no boundaries. But at the same time randomness results in the beauty of a tree, a flower, and a mountain valley.

For in fact how can things be determined or not? If they were determined little if nothing could exist except perhaps raw matter. But if things were undetermined then the world would be like an atomic clock that keeps no time at all.

The claim is made that God creates the complexity of the world, but if God is determinate then God can create nothing. And if God is not determinant then how can we call it God at all?

But if God is this randomness or even if randomness is that which the atheistic scientists take refuge in we must admit it is a mystery and it cannot be understood using induction or deduction. It cannot be solved, described or understood except as something beyond description beyond understanding. This thing is this mystical thing then we can call God or not.

For randomness can explain determinism and freedom at the same time, at least in some sense. Physicality is driven by physical laws but these laws are part of a random process. The mind too is dependent on the physical structure of the brain and is free in that while it is bound by physical, chemical and biological laws these laws ultimately are random in nature. This then provides a basis for the unity of mind and body.

At least we can not say why the world is structured as it is or why we think as we do except to say that we believe things but we can't really say why in an ultimate sense. This too is the crux of the mystical.

When we talk about the meaning of life we find that there is no meaning. Or maybe there is. In Aristotle's law of the excluded middle the wall is destroyed and the meaning of life becomes a mystery and is unfathomable.

So what is randomness? Is it God? We do know that that which is random is unbounded. Its power cannot be understood. It is beyond human conception and may even be perfect in its freedom. Some might call it God those of a religious bent. A philosopher might call it the dogma which drives existence and the scientist might call it simply the unknown or even the unknowable.

Let's think about randomness or rather lets not. For it cannot be thought about anymore than we can understand the basis for our own thoughts. Yet randomness informs us and at the same time drives us and at the same time makes us free.

The Manifest of the Randomness

The randomness drives all, but the randomness also sits in repose. Is this randomness a substitute for God or Being? Is the randomness conscious? Is there intentionality in creation?

One may wonder how randomness may be intentional. Randomness has no pattern and yet perhaps can be thought of as a pattern in itself.

Is there only one way to be random? If this is so then randomness would seem to be determined. Or if there is some finite way that randomness can be then it would seem as well that randomness can be defined but can something that has no order or pattern be defined? Lastly there may be infinite ways of being random, that there are infinite possibilities. If this is true then the example used previously of the random nature of Pi or the random assortment of prime numbers are only singular aspects of randomness.

But of course 7 and 11 are prime while numbers 8 and 4 are not and therefore the types of randomness seem limited, certainly not infinite or even bounded but actually in this case of a determinate nature at least in principle. Or look at the universe. There is a determined rate of change in a falling object, the boiling point of water and molecular structure of water. How can such determined things result from something that seems to be strictly random?

How can we determine the why and how of the determinate physical laws of the universe? Are the laws determinate at all aspects of cosmic creation? Are the physical laws dependent for example on the stage of the big bang? I have read that physical laws differ at the moment of the cataclysmic explosion of the big bang but in our day to day lives physical laws don't differ. But this seems to preclude deciding that this example demonstrates the randomness of physical laws.

Not only is there the question of how physical laws would change based on the evolutionary moment of the universe but the question too can be raised as to if the universe was created again would it have the same physical laws? If so this too could be evidence for some determinate structure.

Do physical laws vary based on the physical size examined? If we look at super-atomic realities and compare them against sub-atomic realities do the physical laws differ? Atoms themselves may follow the standard laws of physics but do quarks? How about anti-matter? These sorts of questions can be asked in the discipline of philosophy although a cosmologist would be more able to describe the physical laws under these circumstances mathematically.

Perhaps the states of physical laws are such that the randomness can manifest. A free play of randomness depends on the physical structure of all. That is perhaps the physical laws of the universe are part of the randomness having an attribute of that where infinity can manifest its free play of all. This sort of adjunct hypothesis to the idea that the randomness determines all is in itself difficult to determine.

Changing the subject a bit one could say that the myriad manifestation of matter, form, and life demonstrates the existence of a cosmic intelligence. But it seems like this cosmic intelligence knows no bounds and the nature of things find themselves in a constant state of transformation in themselves with creations of new realities. This cosmic intelligence is nothing like human intelligence which knows limits, so to attribute the existence of the varieties of things to an omniscient being would be nothing like limited human intelligence. So the question is asked why attribute it to a human like intelligence at all. To call something as the result of intelligent design posits a sort of homunculus which sits in this divine being that directs the creative manifestations of all. How else could this creative intelligence exist if it were not separate?

159

But if this homunculus drives all things infinitely then it too must have something that drives it so we are forced into an infinite regress without an original cause. Something cannot be creative and infinite at the same time although looking at such things as being both may be epistemologically useful.

But the randomness knows no bounds. We can't call that which is random determined any more than we can call that which is random as being simply free. That which is determined is not random and that which is free is free of some bounds but there are no bounds in an existence driven by the seeming structure or structurelessness of the randomness. So randomness is very different from a personal God like Yahweh or even a God like the Indian Brahman. In Indian thought one depends on the trinity of Being, Consciousness and Bliss. Randomness explains Being or existences, consciousness being a manifestation of the ability to choose (i.e., as in humans choosing) in an open system that results from the random nature of existence. And out of this comes the beauty and variety of a healthy ecologic like cosmos.

If something is random then anything is possible. Only through this infinity of possibilities can we have the infinity of nature and all its beautiful incentricities. This beauty can perhaps be talked about as the bliss or delight of All.

But this does not posit an infinite being a God that is beyond our understanding. We dwell in the midst of it all so how can we talk about that which transcends us and surmounts us? This runs in contradiction to the traditional position in Indian thought that the true reality is the island of the spirit which is more real than the matter of the mundane world.

This does not eliminate the possibility of infinity in our own backyard. Things can be infinitely small and infinitely large. The universe can be our surrounding or carry on forever in the distance. But based on these facts we would agree that there are some things that seem to be unknowable but that is no reason to posit a spiritual realm that is more real than the earthly realm and that this spiritual realm drives us.

But as an epilogue is the fact that the infinite does not depend on a supernatural realm but simply a particular aspect of the All which is driven by this randomness and gives all existence the free play of the All. This although does not necessarily deny infinity.

Matter, Energy and Spirit

What is nothing? It seems that nothing is empty space. One may assert that space is not nothing because space is "spatial" but the thing that makes it so are points of reference – material reference.

Space by itself is not spatial without frames of reference. Ultimately without frames of reference nothing could be spatial because there would be no frame of reference including life itself. Like a blind person watching the sunrise or a deaf person hearing birds chirp is meaningless. What could be closer to nothingness than nothing without any frame of reference? But perhaps nothingness is no more nothing than an unobserved sunrise or the unheard chirping of a bird. All are meaningless except perhaps to the bird.

But if you have endless space then there is nothing to define it. And if you have infinite matter there is nothing to delineate it. Space gives a context for matter and delineates matter, that is forms its boundaries, its density and its composition. If you have infinite matter or infinite space you still have nothing in either case.

Energy seems to be a horse of a different color but we already know from Einstein that matter and energy are equivalent in some manner. Matter becomes energy as the sun demonstrates. But what is spirit?

Spirit is not space. No geist lives a matterless existence. One should not fear ghosts.

So in manifestation matter is inseparable from space and space is defined by matter. Spaceless matter is impossible if you look at matter from a sub-atomic perspective. Matter has composition, electrons spinning around through space, gravitation forces pulling and pushing.

All matter is in motion at the subatomic level whether it is living matter or inert matter, whether the structures are carbon based or otherwise. Where does spirit come into it?

The traditional definition of spirit was a medieval attempt to assert the superiority and therefore the moral prerogatives of the human species. While matter appeared to be driven by physical forces, only the geist or spirit was free. But in the world we never see spirit separate from matter empirically. But we are not reduced to determined robots.

Thought is spirit, we are spirit, all life is spirit and also but not obvious everything that exists is spirit. The forces that drive existence drive matter or its consort energy which is all spirit. We cannot make hard distinctions between as Kant called it the self (noumena) and the external (phenomena). All is one.

But this does not posit a sort of pantheism. Something transcends nature. How else can the unexplained be understood? How can something both create and exist at the same time? How can we have self-knowledge and experience at the same time?

Without dwelling on the obvious the self-reflexive nature of randomness drives the uncertain course of history.

Being Consciousness and Bliss are the attributes of the All. The reflective nature of God makes existence possible. Only through existence can anything be known. Only through self-will can we rise up and be free. Only through consciousness can we be united with the One. And only through giving up suffering can we reach an enlightened state of being.

<u>Why Here Now?</u>

As we are born so must we die. But right at this moment we are alive.

One can say that we wouldn't know things at all if we weren't here to perceive them. It seems normal to think that we see things because we are in fact here to see them. Of course if we weren't here then we wouldn't see things at all. So why do we see things? To answer this one must consider what in fact we see.

One thing we know for certain is that things exist or at least seem to in the world. This seems a very safe bet. But would things exist if we weren't here to perceive them? This lies at the crux of the idealistic versus the materialistic position. An idealist would say that if a thing is not perceived then it cannot be said to exist, or an even stronger position might be to assert that if a thing is not perceived it does not exist at all.

If Joe over there does not see the bus hurling toward him and therefore does not know to step out of the way, rest assured that when the bus strikes him he is going to be seriously injured whether he knows it's coming or not. If you are an observer you know as you watch helplessly as Joe walks right into the path of the bus that he is going to be seriously hurt. But what if you didn't know it?

Well Joe would certainly know if the bus hit him whether I observed or not regardless of whether I observed it, if not immediately then while he recovered at the hospital. But what if Joe was not struck by the bus? What if the bus barreled on its way without incident?

The passengers would know the bus was moving but let say as a hypothetical that this bus was run on tracks electronically without a driver and no one was aboard. Does the bus still exist? It seems in principle that even if no one sees the bus move along the tracks that the bus still does move down the tracks. But can we really know this? What if this hypothetical bus never took a passenger and was never observed on its route or at the beginning station or the end station? We would still feel pretty certain the bus did in fact traverse the space between the stations but we can never know for sure can we? But in this case we know it has so we can feel certain that it in fact has.

But if no one is able to know about the journey of bus then we don't really have any way of knowing that the bus actually did make this trip. Let say in our hypothetical bus there are no maintenance records, no engine overhauls and no new coats of paint? Can we still say the bus exists?

This would be like saying that my friend Marlene is my favorite Martian. No one has ever seen a Martian, there is no evidence that Mars could support Martian life, we have no documented incidences of alien spacecraft flying through the sky (well we don't know for sure if UFO's are manned by Martians, maybe Neptunian's). So if I went to you and claimed that our mutual acquaintance Marlene was a Martian you would most likely think I'm nuts and you would probably be right.

In order for us to know an event occurred or to even make the claim that such a thing is possible it must be something that has been verified somehow whether it be by direct observation or by second hand accounts about something that must in some manner be similar to the expected outcome. Otherwise not only would we have no evidence to assert that something occurred but it would probably not even be something that would occur to us personally.

We can even take this a step farther. What if we could arbitrarily construct a universe without humans or animals or even perhaps plants? But on this jagged rock ground sat a bus. Would you still claim the bus was there if nothing was there to observe it? To try to drive (pardon the pun) the point home can you imagine

165

an unobserved bus? What would a bus that was never observed look like? This is of course a contradiction. We cannot know anything about something empirically unless it is in fact observed. It is meaningless to talk about something that is never observed as being observable. It is like trying to hear a sound without your eardrum or for a blind person trying to see the sunrise.

So if we observe the world it is because we are sentient beings and for no other reason. Without our sensory apparatus not only would we not perceive the world but the way in which the world is known would be inaccessible as well. If there was no one else to perceive the world then the world would not demonstrate these attributes that are only known to the senses and in fact are ultimately constructions of the senses. To take an extremely skeptical position we can only know for sure that we exist, we only have self-experience ourselves and do not directly experience anyone else. Everything else we know we experience outside ourselves we know through our own senses. This point seems abundantly clear when one considers Locke's theory of perception.

Without an observer it makes no sense to make a claim about matter. Without sensation it makes no sense to make a claim about matter. Am I claiming then that everything is just spirit? Perhaps everything exists because of God as Berkeley says. But in fact it seems we can have knowledge of the external world. All we really know is that if something that exists in the world changes then this thing can be known (potentially) through the senses. It is potentially for example that dogs can hear high frequencies but humans cannot or bats can understand mass through echoes (e.g., hearing) which is counterintuitive to how humans hear. This then grounds me in materialism but since matter is spirit this does not constitute a problem with my theory. I suppose empiricism could be a way of understanding and comprehending spirit.

As I've claimed in other posts matter and spirit are indivisible. We known through nuclear fission and fusion that matter is just

166

pent up energy. The spark in our brain is no different in essence than the neuronal synapses that crisscross it.

Just as matter cannot be known to exist if it is not observed through the mind or spirit, spirit cannot exist devoid of a universe of matter. Without matter there is nothing. Spirit is not disembodied any more than matter is spiritless. Space makes change possible, matter makes change unavoidable. In order for there to be change in the world there must be interplay between space and matter and the forces that drive matter with its potential energy. As Einstein proved matter can be converted to energy, and as evidenced by the big bang energy can drive the material formation of universes and their developing planets. The error comes from looking at matter as something hard and dumb rather than containing the physical potential for stellar evolution and the birth of life. All is spirit.

So getting back to where we started. Right at the moment we are alive. We see things in the world but why are we here to see it? Well if we weren't here to see it it wouldn't be known by us at all, so it's not surprising that we see as we see it here. Also if the world didn't exist as it is (i.e., sunlight, water, trees etc.) then of course we wouldn't exist lacking in ourselves the stuff of life. Our existence is a testament to the world. We are matter and spirit and our life comes out of our material nature which holds a covert spirit or rather is the same in essence to a covert spirit. When we talk about spirit we are not talking about the disembodied as an assortment of demons and hobgoblins as Sri Aurobindo claims at one point.

According to Hinduism all is Brahman. The inner Brahman is Atman but that too is Brahman. Ultimately we can make no distinction between ourselves and the world because we and the world are one. The ultimate Brahman is indescribable. Thou Art That!

For as Brahman is all all must exist as it is and contrariwise although not necessarily in its present state, and we all live our lives coming to know what is is. Like the skeptic, quietude seeps in because the All cannot be known and ultimately can only be experienced. This is the root of tranquility.

The Yoke

Yoga means "to yoke." This is not simply a Hindu concept but can be applied to study worldwide. There is an essence that "yokes" together all things. Things cannot be reduced to matter as the materialists would like. As is clear matter cannot exist without space nor space without matter.

The European and the East Asian worldviews seem diametrically opposed. The European prefers matter as that which is truly real while the many traditional Asian accounts views matter as illusion or at least not what is essential. The Asian view is that there is something uncreated while in the West the universe is here because of creation. When one in the West talks about creation they are talking about the creation of material that is the material universe. This materialist ideology with its creation myths leads to a world devoid of a prehistory of creation. The earth is created and things appear.

This orientation toward the world leads to a very linear mindset. The past is past and the future is to come. This outlook leads to a very narrow view of the universe where life on other worlds may seem unlikely because of human self-centeredness. This linearity does not allow for other points of origin like a line in geometry with a point of origin which has no width and infinite length away from the point of origin. Its path is unique and can only be followed by itself.

In the Asian tradition on the other hand the material qualities of the world are not entities in themselves, but rather are part of a larger picture that is not bound to the cosmos. The universe largely and the world in particular is thought of as illusion in Hinduism or mutually dependent in Buddhism, or part of a homeostatic bond with pure potentiality as in Taoism. Matter in Asian thought (with the exception of Islam which is tied in with creationist impulses of

169

the Abrahamic tradition) is thought to be non-essential to the ultimate in some way. In these traditions its true nature is misunderstood because of one's limited perspective.

Sri Aurobindo tries to untie the Gordian Knot between matter and spirit. Both perspectives seem to exclude the other but neither can exist on its own! If spirit or God is infinite then matter must exist to form spirit's root. For what is infinity without existence, and what is existence without matter? Matter on the other hand exists and bounds the world. For what is matter without an end, and what is end without a beginning again?

The bounded and the boundless are part of the same Being. It should not seem so strange that they both exist because they cannot exist without each other. While this teaching may seem unfathomable how can it be otherwise?

The Reflexive Nature of Randomness

A common problem is to explain the diversity in the universe. Often times the theists use this diversity as demonstrating an intelligent creator. This seems to be circular reasoning, to explain the antecedent by the consequent which depends on the consequent for its explanation.

Also the problem of the homunculus where God drives the universe in which intelligence in God drives God and an intelligence in the intelligence that drives God which drives the universe and so on. Of course the idea is that God is something that drives itself but this explanation reeks of anthropomorphism. God freely acts as humans supposedly do through an intelligence, albeit an intelligence beyond comprehension but still a self directing Being similarly as humans supposedly are driving the world.

Because of this and other weakness' in a theistic theory of the all Darwinism is looked at as such a threat. With Darwin' theory one doesn't need God or so scientists seem to claim. At the very least God may have created the world but is not actively involved in its unfolding, or rather there is no reason to posit the necessity of God in the universe even though it is conceivable that God is guiding history but only in an ancillary position attached to natural selection.

But does natural selection explain the diversity in the universe? One example, when talking about 100 monkeys typing is that if enough time passes by and the monkeys type long enough at random they will type the complete works of Shakespeare (not through any intelligence of their own but through sheer chance). But it seems we would be waiting longer than the age of the universe for such random forces to determine its awesome complexity.

171

So this is evidence for a Holy Creator? How do things morph over time and result in an ever changing environment in each new age unique and new organisms and the extinction of others?

Nietzsche talks about an organizing principle in the randomness of the universe. But what is the nature of this randomness? One question that occurs to me is is there only one way to be random? Perhaps a mathematician can answer this and if so can you please tell me the answer?

Perhaps there is more than one way to be random but how can we know? If approaching infinity there is derived some sort of pattern (e.g., a "pattern" indicating redundancy) how will we ever know for sure if there is no pattern if we can never arrive at infinity? This rests on the assumption that like Xeno always taking a half step to the wall repeatedly will never arrive at it. This is a better outcome than if the infinite can never be approached because you could never get closer to infinity because it is "without limit" and therefore one could not assess the likelihood in principle of having a non-redundant random string. But this seems counterintuitive for how could anything be known about strings at all if one can't at least in principle approach infinity? It seems clear we can observe redundancy in the world.

Also it seems likely that if strings are infinite then there is only one random string or at least it seems to approach infinity that is the possibility of it not being random would become more apparent as it approached infinity. In other words non-random strings would be eliminated over infinite time as their contradictions became apparent. An infinite number of non-random strings seem counterintuitive if for no other reason than how could one random course be followed over another?

So assuming the universe is infinite over time and space (it seems inconceivable it could be otherwise) then it seems likely that when approaching infinity there would become one random string. Is there a reason for believing there are a limited number of seemingly random strings till one approaches infinity? Well if they are non-random then it is clear that they will result in a contradiction as one approaches infinity.

It seems likely there is only one random string. For how could we say there are 5 random strings? This would be putting a limitation on them which does not exist in the strings themselves that is assuming such a thing could be known at all. But if there are an infinite number of random strings then how could they be differentiated from the finite non-random strings? In other words if there is a finite number of non-random strings then how could there be randomness and non-randomness in the same universe, with the non-random finite and the number of random strings infinite? One might think it's the other way around.

Another possibility can be asserted, that all strings are finite but then we are back at the problem of the monkeys typing a billion years to finally finish Shakespeare. It's a fine piece of work but the universe is so much more.

If there were 5 infinite strings how could they be different from the remaining non-random strings (whose number approaches infinity but arrive at contradictions soon enough)? Why 5, or not 10 or 1000 or a number approaching infinity? This number 5 implies a characteristic of determinateness which is in direct opposition to randomness. So it seems likely that such a thing is not possible.

But does this make one infinite string as the only conclusion? All non-random strings are not possible; therefore a limited number (e.g., more than one) of random strings are not possible. This leaves one random string.

But what is this random string? Is it limited in size, shape? Does it walk around on all fours or stand erect or sit in the sky?

One thing we can say about this random string is that it demonstrates no intelligent design. For when we think of intelligence we think of something that is determinant with a goal

173

in sight. But the universe seems to have no overarching goal. There is no evidence that the universe is here to serve man. It might appear that way because we have water and air and food. But of course we may be confusing the cause for the effect. We are here because there is water and air and food or rather we have "evolved " in this way because of the existence of these needs or more concisely as the interplay of humans and nature. Rest assured that if oxygen was not present neither would we. Perhaps we would be another form but of course if we are different than we are then we will not be ourselves at all. So our existence is because these elements exist, they do not exist to be at our service. This would seem to indicate that there is no purpose in life. But nevertheless we are in the here and now so we might ask why?

Of course if things are truly infinite in "design" then randomness must be infinite as well. And the only way that a string can be infinite is if it is random. A non-random string always results in contradiction. And as I've already proved only one string can exist. Actually when I talk about strings this is another way of talking about the nature of change. I am claiming that change is random. And if change were not random we would be back at our typing monkeys, which have been shown to be impossible.

QED there is one random "string" and this randomness enables a universe that is unlimited contrary to positing a divine intelligence.

An Explanation of History and the Impossibility of Prophecy

For us to think we must be free. Thinking implies free agency. But whether we are free or not seems to be reduced to a matter of semantics. Since we are determined in our randomness then determination about being free or not becomes irrelevant.In order to understand this we must realize that we are matter and spirit, or rather matter is spirit, or rather spirit seems to be concealed in matter. Once one makes a distinction between matter and spirit their definition becomes impossible and we are reduced to many errors. For if we posit matter and spirit as independent entities then we find that they must always be separate in their manifestation which makes freedom impossible.

To be free implies free agency. Therefore it is impossible to know the future and those that claim to be able to do so are charlatans.

Removing the hard distinction of spirit and matter helps to explain human history and the debate about whether there is a difference between Marx and Hegel becomes irrelevant. Also looking at history as being both deterministic and at the same time embracing the class struggle view according to Marx is resolved. For if it is necessary that the world will one day become unified as the proletariat then one need not act because one day it will just become true. This unfortunate byproduct can result apathy certainly something Marx wanted to avoid. On the other hand if we are free in our actions in bringing on the age of the proletariat then such an outcome is not necessary and the promise of heaven on earth may always be delayed and denied, another outcome Marx would not embrace. This is not necessarily an attack on Marx's strategy.

Hegel's logic, the basis for Marx's theory of historical materialism is made relevant when one realizes that history is the result of random forces. Hegel's logic is where there is an existing logic in the world that moves from a position of homeostasis to a position of conflict and then subsequently to a resolution in which what comes about is that which is a new world that never was before.

One needs not to be reductionistic with Hegel's logic. While a resolution may come about based on the nature of the conflict between forces, the world is never again the same and this outcome is different from what existed before. And when conflict comes again the outcome will be different still and are all subsequent transition. So in Hegel we have an element of a deterministic nature but at the same time from resolution to resolution the outcome cannot be predicted. This fact leaves room for Marx and in fact forms the foundation for Marx's historical determinism view and his class struggle view. It should be remarked here that Hegel did not predict the future but described the world in Toto.

A more radical claim is made when one realizes that to make a distinction between Hegel and Marx based on Hegel's spirit and Marx's matter become irrelevant. Hegel's position in the phenomenology of Spirit is ultimately the same as Marx's theories of material relations because matter is spirit and spirit is matter. While this seems contradictory in the West no other solution is possible therefore it must be true ipso facto.

A distinction between the forces that drive history whether they are the ideas of men or the physical nature of change both depend on the random nature of Being which eviscerates this dichotomy. Like the minds of humans so the species are determined in their randomness. Darwin's physical survival of the fittest is little different from Hegel's "spiritual" transitions or Sri Aurobindo's spiritual evolution and are more different semantically than practically.

Only through randomness is the multivariate nature of existence possible. Whether we call this randomness God or not really is not the issue and is ultimately immaterial in this case. Only through randomness can we have the endless nature of change and the infinite possibilities in the world. This may seem counter-intuitive but what else could be possible?

The Epistemology of Metaphysics

I have criticized western epistemology in the past. I have claimed it is a practical truth but has no basis in reality. Descartes dualism has been instrumental in the growth of modern science. But like Buddhism, western science ignores metaphysics. They do this not so much because there is no ultimate reality but rather to know it or not is a waste of time. As the Buddha says one need not know the composition of the arrow, it's poison, where it was shot, or who shot it but to know that one must pull the arrow out.

Science is similar to this in that it is more important to know what is practical rather than what is ultimate. Take for example our technocracy where the practicality of a product depends on its efficacy. Knowing how to do things is more important than to know how things are.

One major criticism I have leveled against western style epistemology is that it ignores our connection with the world. Perhaps this connection is largely ignored because it has been so hard to understand, especially in the West where we have a radical form of individualism. While it cannot be denied that the world and the universe for that matter is composed of different structures and laws, it cannot be denied that we live within these laws and among its structures.

Without accepting our connectedness to things and even denying our dependence on the worlds matter, in particular its biological, chemical, ecological, radiological and gravitational processes is a grave error. One result of taking the position of what I will call hyperindividualism is that there is no regard for anything but the self. In the most extreme cases one only considers ones immediate family if one exists of husband, wife and children. But for some at least even one spouse and siblings may be of less

178

concern. Certainly there is little concern of one's fellow human especially in the highly individualistic societies such as the USA.

Without regard for others of ones own species much less regard for our place in the universe leads to environmental degradation, wars and other crimes result. But this is not a reason to invalidate the Descartean perspective on dualism. For example if one explodes a nuclear bomb to annihilate and enemy, while this act is a crime against those attacked the fact that it performs its function of irradiation of this populace through fission or fusion shows that the atomic theory or "knowledge" is correct. In the same way that our knowledge of the world results in our being good caretakers or exploiters depends more on our ability to take care or exploit, not on the result of our care or exploitation. So as foul as we may see environmental devastation and the like this is not in principle a sufficient reason to say that Descartean scientific epistemology is somehow flawed. So if we make the claim that we "should" protect the environment we are relying on a moral claim which has no bearing on the legitimacy of the Descartean epistemological position. While there may be and I believe are legitimate moral reasons to protect the environment or not bomb your neighbor this says nothing about the epistemological position that underpins such actions, in fact the results from the knowledge we have may even bolster these heinous actions.

Common in today society is the idea that if it works or is "useful" then it contains the attribute of "truth." For if something didn't work in the world then it is not in conformity with the structure of the world which makes these things possible. Fortunately though this is just one attribute or definition of truth.

Truth can also be thought of as becoming aware of the way things are. This is what I have called the "revealing theory of truth." If one is ignorant of the true nature of things then they cannot possess the truth about it. A simple example might be someone who you consider a friend who in fact turns out to be a toady. When we become aware that this person is a toady we then are able to apprehend the true nature of that person where we dwelt under an "illusion" previously. One can think of many examples of solving such mysteries in the stories of Sherlock Holmes. The same sort of thing can be said about metaphysics. One living in the world may think for example that they are separate from their neighbor but in fact they are not and that to think so they dwelt under what the Indians call the veil of Maya. This veil of Maya is not some barrier to our understanding of the spiritual realm but rather simply is in itself our ignorance. When one is ignorant one cannot see, because why? It is because they are ignorant! Once the truth of the matter is apprehended then the veil is lifted. This seems to be similar to what Heidegger is talking about when he discusses "aletheia" in his theories on art.

While there are other theories of truth these two seem most appropriate in describing the difference between epistemology and metaphysics: That which is practical is something technocratic based on laws, principles and axioms, and that which is real is based on apprehension of things as they are in themselves and a more generalized understanding of the nature of all which I call metaphysics. While there are universal principles which are used in sciences such as physics to describe the nature of physical laws, these laws are ultimately a description of how things behave rather than being about their membership in that which is part or all of these physical laws individually and universally in a sense circumscribing Being.

So how can I say that there is something faulty in epistemology and something veritable in metaphysics? Well it seems clear that I cannot say that at all. When thinking about science we are using the tools of induction and deduction. As I have stated before is that empiricism is based on observation and is therefore inductive. The laws of physics are derived from the manipulation of higher mathematics. While the data gathered is basic to observation and

180

known inductively the laws that are derived are known deductively. As I have noted previously they both fail. Empiricism because it is based on observation that cannot be known to be necessarily true (e.g., as Hume proves) and therefore one cannot get a complete picture of the world, and deduction cannot know the true nature of a "thing" first off because knowing a "thing" is based on observation and secondly because the way of understanding that the nature of things are infinite at least as far as can be known and therefore that which is deductive is incomplete. This then is the major limitation with modern science and its adjunct technocracy. Without rehashing the mind/body problem this seems to pose an insurmountable problem for western epistemology.

But epistemology is not necessarily contrary to metaphysics. We can have knowledge about the world and still be part of it. We can look at and water a tree to make it grow and also know that the basic stuff or matter of the tree is composed of by all things. But hyperindividuality will not allow this. The question is why?

In capitalistic societies hyperindividualism has been used to justify class distinctions. Ultimately the efforts of the "individual" determine their wealth and status. There is also another byproduct of hyperindividualism and that is that a class society is the normal nature of things. Darwinism has been reduced to a justification of the lonely death of the homeless or the genocide of the Native Americans. So this sort of hyperindividualism is the root of sexism, racism and classism. It is largely justified by the ruling class as a way to dumb down the less fortunate and justify the rich's own prerogatives. It's no accident that we value liberty more than property as being the equalizing factor between rich and poor. For liberty in itself says nothing about who should possess property but rather when talking about liberty we are talking about how some individual can enjoy the freedom to choose. This reminds me of the adage that a "bum" may be forced to sleep in the

181

park because of destitution but the bum is free to sleep in any park they like. Well perhaps with the disappearance of our other rights this is disappearing too.

We can both look out and look in. But because of greed or sloth this position is rejected. Rather we are grounded in an other worldly perspective where the world we live is inconsequential.

Only through realizing the limitations and errors in our thinking can we be persuaded to adopt more cogent practices. Even more important is to experience life and cultivate a conscious appreciation for our lives as we are here for tomorrow may be too late.

www.ingramcontent.com/pod-product-compliance
Lightning Source LLC
Chambersburg PA
CBHW070955040426
42443CB00007B/513